Measuring Welfare Changes and Tax Burdens

This book is dedicated to the memory of Kath Creedy

Measuring Welfare Changes and Tax Burdens

John Creedy

*The Truby Williams Professor of Economics,
University of Melbourne, Australia*

Edward Elgar

Cheltenham, UK • Northampton, MA, USA

Published by
Edward Elgar Publishing Limited
8 Lansdown Place
Cheltenham
Glos GL50 2HU
UK

Edward Elgar Publishing, Inc.
6 Market Street
Northampton
Massachusetts 01060
USA

A catalogue record for this book
is available from the British Library

Library of Congress Cataloguing in Publication Data

Creedy, John, 1949-
    Measuring welfare changes and tax burdens / John Creedy.
    1. Welfare economics. 2. Taxation. I. Title.
    HB846.C74   1998
    336.2–dc21   98–17082
                                                        CIP

ISBN 1 85898 921 3

Printed and bound in Great Britain by MPG Books Ltd, Bodmin, Cornwall

Contents

III Applications

List of Figures

List of Tables

Acknowledgements

Chapters 3 and 4 are based on work that was originally supported by the New Zealand Treasury though, of course, the views expressed do not necessarily represent those of the Treasury. I am very grateful to Tom Hall and Geoff Lewis for helpful discussions, particularly relating to material in chapter 4. Chapters 5 and 6 are based respectively on Creedy (1998b) and Creedy (1998a). Chapter 9 is based on Creedy and van de Ven (1997); chapter 10 is based on joint work carried out with Robert Dixon and reported in Creedy and Dixon (1997, 1998); chapter 11 is based on material in Cornwell and Creedy (1996, 1997). I am very grateful to my joint authors, as well as the editors of the relevant journals, for permission to use the material here. Valuable support has also been provided in the form of Research Grants from the University of Melbourne Faculty of Economics and Commerce, as well as Small Grants from the Australian Research Council. Research assistance was also provided at various stages by Nahid Khan, Cameron Martin and Justin van de Ven. Valuable editorial help was also given by my wife, Kath. This book was substantially completed when Kath died, and it is to her that it is dedicated.

Part I

Introduction

Chapter 1

Introduction and Outline

In many contexts it is required to know the effects on the welfare of well-specified population groups of changes in the prices of goods and services and of changes in wage rates. It is particularly important to be able to measure the changes in terms of money units, which can easily be added over consumers. In many cases the changes in prices arise as a result of the introduction of a tax or a change in commodity or income taxation. Often it is required to examine the likely effects of alternative hypothetical tax regimes. The distortion to consumer behaviour that is produced by taxation gives rise to the concept of the excess burden of taxation; even if individuals have their tax payments returned to them, there remains a welfare loss.

This book is concerned with some of the conceptual and practical problems of measuring welfare changes and excess burdens arising from taxation. It has two broad aims. The first aim is to provide an introductory review of alternative concepts and practical approaches to measurement. This is not intended to be comprehensive or to be entirely rigorous, but tries to be accessible to a wide range of economists. The second broad aim is to provide a number of practical examples of welfare analyses in a variety of contexts.

The idea of the excess burden of a tax is quite old and, along with those such as opportunity cost and comparative advantage, is a central and non-trivial concept in economics. However, this does not mean that the subject is settled; it continues to give rise to a considerable literature. Indeed, this is not surprising in view of the substantial difficulties involved. It is therefore

1

worth considering whether attempts to measure welfare costs are worthwhile, given the difficulties and the data limitations facing most studies. Could it be said that the study of welfare costs represents the Holy Grail of applied microeconomics, and would it be better to avoid reporting spuriously accurate results that may be substantially influenced by *a priori* assumptions rather than the data used? Are such attempts worse than useless?

It is of course not difficult to find expressions of such nihilistic views. But while the problems should certainly not be minimised, debates regarding tax reforms, particularly those of the non-marginal variety, are necessarily framed in terms of their expected effects on 'equity and efficiency'. In the absence of serious attempts to measure the orders of magnitude involved, any debate will inevitably be influenced instead only by uninformed guesses and rhetoric. It is suggested that careful studies, which make the assumptions clear, stress their limitations and provide a range of sensitivity analyses, can make a valuable contribution to decision-making and the evaluation of alternative tax structures.

1.1   Outline of Future Chapters

The substantive chapters of this book are divided into two parts, consistent with the two broad aims mentioned above. In view of the central role of demand analysis in the analysis of welfare changes, chapter 2, the first chapter of part II, provides a brief review of some of the main results in consumer theory. No attempt is made to provide a comprehensive review or to prove all the results, or even to state them with complete rigour. It aims to provide an informal collection of results that are useful in a variety of contexts, particularly relating to welfare measurement.

There are four types of demand function. These include the pair of Marshallian ordinary and inverse demand curves, and the associated pair of compensated or Hicksian demand and inverse demand curves. In each case the demand curve is associated with a constrained optimisation problem, yet it is possible to avoid the difficulties of working with first-order conditions based on Lagrangians by making use of duality results. The relevant duality results are stressed in chapter 2.

Chapter 3 provides an introduction to various concepts of welfare change, paying particular attention to the measurement issues involved. It does not pretend to be an exhaustive survey of the huge number of contributions to this broad topic, but attempts to pull some of the threads of the literature together. The emphasis is on conceptual issues and approximations designed to reduce the information required for the calculation of welfare changes. It begins by summarising the basic definitions of welfare change, in particular the compensating and equivalent variations, comparing these with the famous Marshallian measure of consumer surplus. It then presents measures of the excess burden arising from taxation that are associated with the different welfare change measures.

The standard measures of welfare change and excess burden involve the expenditure function (giving the minimum cost of reaching a specified indifference curve for a given set of prices) and Hicksian, or compensated, demand curves rather than Marshallian demand curves. The latter are sometimes very misleadingly said to be directly observable. However, the problem immediately arises that calculation of the welfare measures appears to require knowledge of the precise form of utility, and hence expenditure, functions. Several responses to this problem have been adopted. One approach is to use an approximation to the true measure which involves compensated demand elasticities but does not depend on the form of utility functions; these approximations, including the analysis of marginal tax reform, are also examined in this chapter.

Chapter 3 goes on to discuss excess burdens in the special context of income taxation and labour supply variations. This context raises no new fundamental issues, but warrants special attention given the importance of income taxation, and the fact that a change in the net wage rate, the effective price of leisure, has a more complex effect than a change in a typical commodity price.

The treatment of income taxation leads to the subject of the marginal welfare cost of taxation and of public funds. The excess burden measures are essentially concerned with comparisons of a distortionary tax system with a non-distortionary system, that is lump sum taxation, which is assumed to raise the same revenue. However, increases in taxation from an existing tax-distorted situation are often required in order to raise additional revenue which is used to finance public expenditure. Analysis of this type of 'balanced budget' operation is only similar to the excess burden calculation if the additional public expenditure is equivalent to a cash transfer. Otherwise the expenditure can have important implications for the yield of existing taxes. This also means that, starting from a tax-distorted system, lump sum taxes can affect the ability of existing taxes to collect revenue. This type of consideration leads to the important concept of the 'marginal cost of funds'.

The emphasis of chapter 4 moves from conceptual to empirical measurement issues. Attention is given to methods of producing exact welfare measures. The term 'exact' is used to distinguish measures from approximations, but it is not meant to indicate any special precision. There is also a need to allow for population heterogeneity, since individuals are in different circumstances and face different tax rates. There are two broad approaches to providing an exact measure of welfare change for different population groups. One is to use observed data in order to estimate the required parameters of a specified expenditure function by deriving the associated demand functions; the analytical or formal links between the expenditure functions and the demand functions are explicitly used. The expenditure function may be obtained by first specifying the form of the direct utility function; an example using the linear expenditure system is given. Alternatively the procedure may begin by specifying a form for the indirect utility function; an example using the 'almost ideal' demand system is given.

The second approach involves starting from an estimated form of Marshallian demand curve and moving from this to the required Hicksian demand curve, either by an algebraic method of integration or by a numerical method of integration. These approaches are also discussed in chapter 4. Both the algebraic and numerical integration methods discussed in this section use parametric estimates of consumer demand functions. The *a priori* imposition of some structure makes it easier to estimate demand functions, particularly using a limited amount of data. However, numerical methods of integration can be applied to non-parametric estimates of demand functions, raising no new basic welfare measurement issues; they are therefore not discussed here.

An important concept is that of 'equivalent income'. This measures the income that, at some reference set of prices and wages, gives the same utility as an individual's actual income. It transforms utility into expenditure levels and provides a form of indirect utility function representing the preference ordering. The equivalent income is thus a 'money metric' measure of utility based on the indirect utility function. An overall evaluation of a tax policy change can be achieved using a specified social evaluation, or welfare, function which is evaluated using the distribution of 'equivalent incomes'. The social welfare function makes explicit the decision-maker's willingness to trade equity for efficiency. The use of equivalent incomes in this context is also discussed in chapter 4.

Chapter 5 describes a method of estimating the welfare effects of a set of price changes, based on the use of the linear expenditure system discussed in chapter 4. One serious limitation of the linear expenditure system, when a single set of parameters is used, is that its implications for optimal indirect taxes are very strong, since it gives rise to uniform indirect taxes. However, instead of using a single set of parameters, the approach described in chapter 5 is based on estimates of the linear expenditure system for each of a range of total expenditure groups. Households within each group are assumed to have the same preferences, but these are allowed to vary with total expenditure. The uniformity of optimal indirect taxes does not arise with taste heterogeneity. It is shown how estimates of the parameters of the linear expenditure system can be obtained, for each total expenditure group, using only cross-sectional budget data. The strong *a priori* restrictions underlying this parametric approach represent the cost of obtaining a very large number of demand elasticities with limited data. However, such a data limitation is a situation that faces many researchers who nevertheless need some idea of orders of magnitude in order to examine policy issues.

Chapter 6 turns to the subject of optimal income taxation. The standard approach to the analysis of optimal income taxation involves the maximisation of a social welfare function specified in terms of individuals' utilities. Within this framework it has been found that the optimal linear income tax rate is not very sensitive to the degree of relative inequality aversion of the welfare function. It is, however, sensitive to the elasticity of substitution between leisure and consumption. It appears that the case for high optimal tax rates rests on an assumption of a low elasticity of substitution rather than a high degree of inequality aversion. The implications of using the concept of 'equivalent income' in optimal income tax studies in place of utilities have received little attention. Chapter 6 examines the implications of using each individual's equivalent income in place of utility in the context of the optimal linear income tax. The choice between utility levels or equivalent incomes in the social welfare function involves a value judgement just as the form of welfare function itself involves a value judgement. Hence, it is not the purpose of this chapter to argue that any particular welfare measure should be used in analyses of alternative tax structures. Rather, consistent with the general approach to optimal taxation, the analysis involves exploring the implications of adopting alternative value judgements.

A major finding of chapter 6 is that there is less inequality in utility than in equivalent income, and the marginal social welfare from higher-wage people is lower for utility compared with equivalent income. These two features have opposing effects on the optimal marginal tax. When inequality aversion is very low, the first effect is small and the optimal tax is expected to be lower when using equivalent income compared with utility. Similarly, when inequality aversion is high, the relatively higher inequality of equivalent income dominates and the associated optimal tax is expected to be higher than when utility is used. The net result is that the optimal result is expected to be more sensitive to inequality aversion when using equivalent income than when using utility in the social welfare function.

Part III turns to applications. The examples given in part III cover only a very small range of the many possible types of application of methods of welfare analysis. In addition, they are limited by a paucity of data regarding price responses, so that reliance has been placed on the use of cross-sectional budget data and the use of strong assumptions regarding the link between price and income elasticities. However, it is hoped that they provide a glimpse of the sort of welfare study that is possible. Each chapter in part III has been written so that it can be read independently. This inevitably involves a small amount of repetition.

Part III begins in chapter 7 with an analysis of marginal indirect tax reform. The calculation of optimal indirect tax rates requires a great deal of information about preferences and demand patterns, which is extremely difficult to obtain even in countries with rich data sources. One response to this problem is to concentrate instead on marginal tax reform, following the type of approach discussed in chapter 3. This allows the same sort of distributional weights as used in optimal tax calculations to be imposed. As in the optimal tax approach, the method considers the implications of adopting a social welfare function specified in terms of individuals' utilities. Chapter 7 examines marginal indirect tax reform in Australia. A special problem is raised because of the fact that there is a large variety of different types of indirect tax, including payroll tax, fringe benefits tax, taxes on property (including financial transactions), sales taxes, excises and levies, taxes on international trade, taxes on gambling and insurance, motor vehicle and franchise taxes. The evaluation of the effect of these taxes on final consumers involves the appropriate allowance for inter-industry transactions.

Chapter 8 turns to the analysis of non-marginal indirect tax reform, and examines the welfare changes imposed on different income (total expenditure) groups by changes in prices which arise from a major change to the system of indirect taxes. The approach is based on the use of the linear expenditure system, as described in chapter 5. The method is used to examine the distributional effects of the change in the indirect tax system in New Zealand during the mid-1980s, carried out as part of a major package of tax reforms involving a flattening of the income tax structure, a large amount of base-broadening and a partial shift towards indirect taxation.

Chapter 9 looks at the welfare effects of inflation. Distributional implications of inflation exist because of the fact that prices do not all change by the same proportion over time. If there is a systematic tendency for the price of those goods which form a relatively higher proportion of the total expenditure of low-income households to increase relatively more than other goods, inflation produces adverse effects on the distribution of real income. The effect of differential price changes on welfare also depends on the extent to which households substitute away from those goods whose prices increase relatively more. Studies of inflation in several countries, using a variety of approaches, have found a small effect of this type.

Chapter 9 examines the redistributive effect of price changes in Australia over the sixteen-year period from 1980 to 1995, and the effects of inflation in New Zealand over the period 1993 to 1995. The distributional effects of inflation are examined in two ways. First, it examines the way in which equivalent variations vary with household income. Secondly, values of several alternative measures of inequality are reported, for a range of degrees of aversion towards inequality. The inequality measures are based on the distribution of equivalent income, defined in chapter 4. The analysis is based entirely on consumption and therefore ignores wealth accumulation and changes in asset prices. The estimates are based on the use of the linear expenditure system, following the approach set out in chapter 5.

The aim of chapter 10 is to examine the distributional effects of monopoly. Numerous studies have found relatively small aggregate welfare costs of monopoly, but it is possible that small aggregate welfare losses can coexist with large distributional effects. There seem to have been very few studies of the distributional effects of monopoly, which is regarded more broadly as the absence of competition rather than the existence of a single seller. The analysis is based on a comparison of the actual prices with those that would otherwise be found if all goods were produced under competitive conditions. It requires two basic ingredients. First, it is necessary to have a way of measuring the welfare and distributional effects of a set of proportional price changes. The welfare measures and responses of consumers to price changes are based on the use of the linear expenditure system, as described in chapter 5, and estimated separately for each of a range of income groups. Secondly, it is necessary to specify the counterfactual. In the present context the price changes are the price differences from a comparison of monopoly pricing with prices that would otherwise arise in a competitive market. If commodity prices were to increase by the same proportion, in the hypothetical movement from competition to monopolistic markets, then there would be no distributional effects. The percentage change in the equivalent income of each household would be the same irrespective of its expenditure pattern. However, if the goods which form a larger share of the expenditure of lower-income households typically increase in price by relatively more than other goods, then a measure of inequality would be expected to increase. Such an increase is indeed found in chapter 10.

Chapter 11 turns to the analysis of the effects of a carbon tax. Recognition of the adverse effects of carbon dioxide emissions, resulting mainly from the combustion of fossil fuels, has led to proposals for non-market mechanisms such as regulation, and market mechanisms such as tradable emissions permits and carbon taxes, in order to reduce emissions. Market methods are usually preferred in terms of efficiency and the carbon tax is deemed the easiest to implement and monitor. A carbon tax would affect the price of fossil fuels and thus consumer prices, both directly for fuels and indirectly for manufactured goods. These price changes would alter the levels of final demands, and therefore fossil fuel use and aggregate carbon dioxide emissions. This chapter investigates the orders of magnitude of a carbon tax required to reduce carbon dioxide emissions in Australia such that the Toronto Target is met; this requires a reduction in emissions of 20 per cent of 1988 levels by 2005. It also examines the distributional implications of carbon taxation where allowance is made for consumer responses to price changes and the indirect price effects of taxes. The method focuses on the reduction in emissions resulting entirely from consumer demand responses. However, this chapter also examines the implications of changes in intermediate requirements in the production process, that is, a change in the input-output matrix.

Part II

Theory and Methods

Chapter 2

Review of Demand Analysis

In view of the central role of demand analysis in the analysis of welfare changes, this chapter provides a brief review of some of the main results in consumer theory. No attempt is made to provide a comprehensive review or to prove all the results, or even to state them with complete rigour. It aims to provide an informal collection of results that are useful in a variety of contexts, particularly in welfare economics. For more detailed treatments see, for example, Anderson (1980), Cornes (1992), Deaton (1979), Deaton and Muellbauer (1980), Gravelle and Rees (1992), Varian (1992) and Weymark (1980).

Attention is restricted to single-period models. The foundation of consumer theory is the theory of optimising behaviour, and an important role is played by duality results. Direct and indirect utility functions are examined in sections 2.1 and 2.2. The concepts of expenditure and distance functions are presented in section 2.3, and compensated demand functions are examined in section 2.4. Demand elasticities are presented in section 2.5, which is followed by a brief examination of aggregation over consumers, in section 2.6.

Most of the discussion concerns a single individual, assumed to face prices, p_i, for the ith good $(i = 1, ..., n)$. Where x_i denotes the consumption of good i, and m is the budget, or 'income', then the budget constraint facing the individual is $m \geq \sum_{i=1}^{n} p_i x_i$.

2.1   The Direct Utility Function

The direct utility function is denoted $U(x)$, where U represents a preference ordering of consumption bundles, and is defined up to a monotonic increasing transformation, so that utility is ordinal. For interior, or tangency, solutions maximisation of $U(x)$ subject to the budget constraint, $m = \sum_{i=1}^{n} p_i x_i$, gives the Lagrangian:

$$L = U(x) + \lambda \left(m - \sum_{i=1}^{n} p_i x_i \right) \qquad (2.1)$$

and the $n+1$ first-order conditions are $\partial U / \partial x_i = \lambda p_i$ for $i = 1, ..., n$, along with the budget constraint. These are used in order to determine the quantities consumed and the Lagrange multiplier, λ. For any pair of goods, this means that interior solutions must satisfy:

$$\frac{\partial U / \partial x_i}{\partial U / \partial x_j} = \frac{p_i}{p_j} \qquad (2.2)$$

giving the familiar equi-marginal condition that marginal utility per unit of money devoted to each good, $(\partial U / \partial x_i) / p_i$, must be the same for all goods. This is equivalent to the tangency of an indifference curve with the budget line, shown as follows.

Along an indifference curve:

$$dU = \sum_{i=1}^{n} \frac{\partial U}{\partial x_i} dx_i = 0 \qquad (2.3)$$

Hence, for any pair of goods, the marginal rate of substitution of good i for good j, denoted $MRS_{i,j}$, is:

$$MRS_{i,j} = -\left. \frac{dx_j}{dx_i} \right|_U = \frac{\partial U / \partial x_i}{\partial U / \partial x_j} \qquad (2.4)$$

This gives the tangency condition that the marginal rate of substitution of good i for j, the (absolute) slope of an indifference curve in a diagram with x_j on the vertical axis and x_i on the horizontal axis, is equal to the price ratio, p_i / p_j, which is the (absolute) slope of the budget constraint. This gives the equi-marginal condition stated above. The marginal rate of substitution is obviously not affected by monotonic transformations of $U(x)$.

2.1.1 Homothetic Preferences

A function, $f(x)$ is homogeneous of degree k if $f(\theta x) = \theta^k f(x)$. For linear homogeneous functions, where $k = 1$, differentiation with respect to θ and setting $\theta = 1$ immediately gives Euler's law, $\sum_{i=1}^{n} x_i \frac{\partial f(x)}{\partial x_i} = f(x)$.

Differentiating $f(\theta x) = \theta^k f(x)$ with respect to x_i gives the result that $\partial f(x)/\partial x_i$ is homogeneous of degree $k - 1$. In the linear homogeneous case, then:

$$\frac{\partial f(\theta x)}{\partial x_i} = \frac{\partial f(x)}{\partial x_i} \tag{2.5}$$

In the context of a linear homogeneous utility function, $U(x)$, this implies that marginal utility, and hence the marginal rate of substitution, is constant along a ray from the origin; an equal proportionate increase in all x_i has no effect on the slope of the indifference curves. Hence budget shares are independent of both m and U. This implies that Engel curves are straight lines through the origin and all income elasticities are unity.

These results have important implications for aggregation over individuals. In view of the ordinal nature of utility, it would be undesirable to be restricted to utility functions that are linear homogeneous. However, this property also holds for functions that are positive monotonic transformations of linear homogeneous functions; such functions are known as homothetic functions.

2.1.2 Endowments

Suppose that the individual holds an endowment, s_i, of good i, in addition to the fixed income, m. The budget constraint becomes:

$$\sum_{i=1}^{n} p_i x_i = m + \sum_{i=1}^{n} p_i s_i \tag{2.6}$$

and it is convenient to define 'full income', M, as the budget that is available
if the endowments are converted into money. From the resulting optimal
values of x_i in relation to s_i it is possible to find whether the individual is
a net demander or supplier of the good. In this context an increase in the
price of a good increases the value of the individual's endowment. For a net
supplier of the good, this can therefore produce an increase in demand, or
reduction in supply. This gives rise to a 'backward bending' supply curve,
which in turn creates the possibility of multiple equilibria in exchange models.

A popular context is the case where the individual has an endowment,
H, of time and the net wage rate is w per unit of time. If the utility function
is augmented to include leisure, h, then $U(x, h)$ is maximised subject to the
constraint $\sum_{i=1}^{n} p_i x_i + wh = m + Hw = M$, and the supply of labour is given
by $H - h$. In this case, an increase in the net wage, by increasing the value of
the endowment, may lead to a reduction in labour supply despite the higher
opportunity cost of leisure.

2.1.3   Marshallian Demands

The first-order conditions can in principle be solved to express the demand
for each good as a function of m and the prices, p, giving the Marshallian
demand functions, $x_i^M(p, m)$. These are homogeneous of degree zero, since
$x_i^M(\theta p, \theta m) = x_i^M(p, m)$ and an equal proportional increase in all prices
and income leaves demands unchanged. However, except for some standard
cases, the first-order conditions are too nonlinear to be solved explicitly for
the Marshallian demands.

In some contexts it is appropriate to regard the price, or willingness to
pay for each good, as the endogenous variable. This gives rise to the inverse Marshallian demand function, $p_i^M(x, m)$, which is more easily obtained
from the direct utility function than the ordinary demand function. Multiplying each first-order condition by x_i and summing over all goods gives
$\sum_{i=1}^{n} x_i (\partial U / \partial x_i) = \lambda \sum_{i=1}^{n} p_i x_i = \lambda m$. Solving for λ and substituting into
each first-order condition then gives:

$$p_i^M(x, m) = m \left\{ \frac{\partial U/\partial x_i}{\sum_{j=1}^n x_j (\partial U/\partial x_j)} \right\} \tag{2.7}$$

Hence, the inverse demand function can be expressed in terms of normalised prices, $\tilde{p}_i = p_i/m$, so that:

$$\tilde{p}_i^M(x) = \frac{\partial U/\partial x_i}{\sum_{j=1}^n x_j (\partial U/\partial x_j)} \tag{2.8}$$

This is sometimes referred to as the Hotelling-Wold identity.

2.2 The Indirect Utility Function

Substituting the demands $x_i^M(p, m)$ into the direct utility function gives the indirect utility function, $V(p, m)$, which is also expressed as a function of p and m. The indirect utility function is nondecreasing in m and nonincreasing in p. It is homogeneous of degree zero, so that $V(\theta p, \theta m) = V(p, m)$, implying that an equal proportional increase in prices and income has no effect on utility.

In view of the difficulty of solving for the demands from U, it is often useful to begin the analysis by specifying a form for the indirect utility function. The corresponding indifference curves are given in a diagram in which prices appear on the axes. In terms of normalised prices, $\tilde{p}$, indirect utility can be written as $V = V(\tilde{p})$ and along an indifference curve:

$$dV = \sum_{i=1}^n \frac{\partial V}{\partial \tilde{p}_i} d\tilde{p}_i = 0 \tag{2.9}$$

The minimisation of indirect utility subject to the budget constraint then gives a corresponding tangency solution in terms of the inverse demands, or willingness to pay, expressed as:

$$\frac{\partial V/\partial p_i}{\partial V/\partial p_j} = \frac{x_i}{x_j} \tag{2.10}$$

If the indirect utility function is available, the associated direct utility function can be obtained by solving the problem of finding the prices to minimise $V(p,m)$, subject to the constraint that $\sum_{i=1}^{n} p_i x_i = m$, remembering that $V(p,m)$ is nonincreasing in p. The Lagrangian is thus $L = -V(p,m) + \lambda\left(m - \sum_{i=1}^{n} p_i x_i\right)$, giving $-\partial V(p,m)/\partial p_i = \lambda x_i$, where λ is the Lagrange multiplier for this problem. Solving for the inverse demands, that is the ps, and substituting into $V(p,m)$ gives the direct utility function. However, solving for the inverse demands from the indirect utility function can prove to be intractable, just as solving for the Marshallian demands from the direct utility function is often intractable.

2.2.1   Marshallian Demand Functions

The Marshallian demands are readily obtained from the indirect utility function, just as the inverse Marshallian demands are readily obtained from the direct utility function. Multiplying the first-order conditions by $\tilde{p}_i$ and summing gives $\lambda = -\sum_{i=1}^{n}(\partial V/\partial \tilde{p}_i)\,\tilde{p}_i$, so that substituting for λ gives the Marshallian demand:

$$x_i^M(p,m) = \frac{\partial V/\partial \tilde{p}_i}{\sum_{j=1}^{n}(\partial V/\partial \tilde{p}_j)\,\tilde{p}_j} \qquad (2.11)$$

This is sometimes referred to as the Ville-Roy identity. An alternative form, usually known as Roy's identity, gives the demands as:

$$x_i^M(p,m) = -\frac{\partial V(p,m)/\partial p_i}{\partial V(p,m)/\partial m} \qquad (2.12)$$

This follows from the fact that for fixed V, total differentiation with respect to p_i and m gives $(\partial V/\partial p_i)\,dp_i + (\partial V/\partial m)\,dm = 0$, combined with the requirement that $dm = x_i dp_i$.

2.3   The Expenditure and Distance Functions

2.3.1   The Expenditure Function

Consider the problem of finding the minimum expenditure, $\sum_{i=1}^{n} p_i x_i$, required in order to reach a specified indifference curve or level of utility, U^*, at prices, p. The Lagrangian for this problem is $L = -\sum_{i=1}^{n} p_i x_i + \lambda(U - U^*)$.

This is in fact the dual problem to that of utility maximisation subject to a budget constraint. It is easily seen that the first-order conditions for this problem are precisely the same as with the dual problem of utility maximisation. However, the optimal values of x are expressed in terms of the given level of utility and prices: these are the Hicksian or compensated demands, $x_i^H (p, U)$. Substitution of these demands into $\sum_{i=1}^{n} p_i x_i$ gives the minimum expenditure, expressed also as a function of U and p; this is the expenditure function, $E(p, U)$. This is concave and linear homogeneous in prices, since an equal proportional increase in all prices increases the minimum expenditure required to attain a given level of utility by the same amount; hence $E(\theta p, U) = \theta E(p, U)$.

However, if the indirect utility function $V(p, m)$ is available, the required minimum expenditure is obtained simply by inverting V in order to express m as a function of V and the prices, p, and then replacing V with U and m with $E(p, U)$. More formally, the two useful relationships used here can be stated as $U = V(p, E(p, U))$ and $m = E(p, V(p, m))$. Since $V(p, m)$ is nondecreasing in m, the required inversion can always, at least in principle, be carried out.

The expenditure function can also be used to define a constant-utility price index number, P_U, for price changes from p^0 to p^1, given by:

$$P_U = \frac{E(p^1, U)}{E(p^0, U)} \tag{2.13}$$

The Laspeyres and Paasche forms of this index are defined respectively for pre- and post-change utility.

For a linear homogeneous direct utility function, an equal proportionate increase of θ in all x_i produces a θ-fold increase in utility; for fixed prices, this costs θ times as much. Since utility is ordinal, this result may not be regarded as interesting. However, it suggests that the expenditure function can be written as:

$$E(p, U) = U E(p, 1) = U e(p) \tag{2.14}$$

where $e(p) = E(p, 1)$. Similarly:

$$V\left(p,m\right) = mV\left(p,1\right) = mv\left(p\right) \tag{2.15}$$

The application of Roy's identity then gives the result that Marshallian demand functions are linear in m, with all income elasticities equal to unity. This has implications for aggregation, discussed below. For homothetic preferences, the constant-utility price index number is independent of U.

2.3.2   Money Metric Utility

The expenditure function can be used to define the concept of a 'money metric' utility function. This is motivated by the need for a money measure which, unlike ordinal utility, can be added over consumers. The major candidate is a system of labelling indifference curves based on the cost, at specified prices, of getting on to a specified indifference curve. Such a cost measure is clearly independent of monotonic transformations of the utility function, which simply change the utility index given to each indifference curve.

The money metric utility arises from considering the question of what amount of money an individual would require, at a set of prices, p, in order to be as well-off as when consuming a bundle of goods given by x. The amount, which may be denoted $m\left(p,x\right)$, is given by the money that would place the individual on the same indifference curve that passes through x. Hence it is given directly from the expenditure function in terms of direct utility, since:

$$m\left(p,x\right) = E\left(p,U\left(x\right)\right) \tag{2.16}$$

If x is fixed, then $m\left(p,x\right)$ behaves just like an expenditure function and has the same properties. Alternatively, when p is fixed, $m\left(p,x\right)$ is a monotonic transformation of the direct utility function, and is therefore itself a utility function.

Another money metric can be defined by considering the question of how much money the individual would need, at some reference set of prices, p_r, in order to be as well-off as when facing the prices p and having an income of m.

This amount, denoted $m_e(p_r, p, m)$, is given from the expenditure function in terms of indirect utility, since:

$$m_e(p_r, p, m) = E(p_r, V(p, m)) \qquad (2.17)$$

This behaves just like an expenditure function with respect to variations in p_r for fixed V. However, for fixed p_r it is a monotonic transformation of the indirect utility function. The money metric indirect utility is in some contexts also referred to as 'equivalent income'.

2.3.3 The Distance Function

The function that is 'dual' to the expenditure function is the distance function, $D(x, U)$. This expresses the extent to which each of a set of xs must be adjusted (divided) in order to bring consumption on to a specified indifference curve, associated with utility of U. For given U, say U', and x, suppose the scalar adjustment is denoted by δ. Then $U' = U(x_1/\delta, ..., x_n/\delta)$, so that the solution for δ is given simply by the process of inverting the direct utility function. The distance function is then given by replacing U' with U, and δ with $D(x, U)$. Hence the distance function is obtained by inverting the direct utility function, just as the expenditure function is obtained by inverting the indirect utility function.

The distance function is homogeneous of degree 1 in x, so that $D(\theta x, U) = \theta D(x, U)$. It is increasing (and concave) in x and decreasing in U. It is sometimes referred to as the 'transformation' function.

2.4 Compensated Demands

The expenditure, or cost, function is extremely convenient in demand and welfare analysis when considering the demands as endogenous (depending on price changes), while the distance function is extremely convenient when considering the willingness to pay (or normalised prices) as endogenous. They can be used to obtain the associated compensated or Hicksian demands.

For changes in prices the Hicksian or compensated demands, $x_i^H(p, U)$, that is the demands that occur when changes are restricted to take place along a given indifference curve, have been defined above. They are the solutions to the dual problem of minimising expenditure subject to reaching an indifference curve. However, a valuable result is that they can also be obtained directly from the expenditure function by using Shephard's lemma, such that:

$$x_i^H(p, U) = \frac{\partial E(p, U)}{\partial p_i} \tag{2.18}$$

For unchanged total expenditure when prices change:

$$dE(p, U) = \sum_{i=1}^n (\partial E / \partial p_i) \, dp_i = \sum_{i=1}^n x_i dp_i = 0 \tag{2.19}$$

giving the tangency solution in price space, such that:

$$\left. \frac{dp_j}{dp_i} \right|_E = -\frac{x_i}{x_j} \tag{2.20}$$

A useful pair of results link the Hicksian and Marshallian demands, since:

$$x_i^M(p, m) = x_i^M(p, E(p, U)) = x_i^H(p, U) \tag{2.21}$$

$$x_i^H(p, U) = x_i^H(p, V(p, m)) = x_i^M(p, m) \tag{2.22}$$

The Hicksian demand at U is therefore the same as the Marshallian demand at income $E(p, U)$, and the Marshallian demand at m is the same as the Hicksian demand at $V(p, m)$.

2.4.1   Inverse Demands

The compensated, or Hicksian, inverse demands, $\tilde{p}_i^H(x, U)$, that is the willingness to pay for goods when changes are restricted to take place along a given indifference curve (with normalised prices on the axes), can be obtained from the distance function, just as the compensated demands are obtained from the expenditure function. Shephard's lemma can again be used, whereby:

$$\tilde{p}_i^H(x,U) = \frac{\partial D(x,U)}{\partial x_i} \tag{2.23}$$

This result is sometimes referred to as the Shephard-Hanoch lemma. The compensated inverse demands are homogeneous of degree zero in x, so that $\tilde{p}_i^H(\theta x, U) = \tilde{p}_i^H(x, U)$. Hence, associated with each level of U and with a set of quantity *ratios,* there is a set of expenditure-normalised 'shadow prices'. For unchanged total utility when consumption changes:

$$dD(x,U) = \sum_{i=1}^{n}(\partial D/\partial x_i)\, dx_i = \sum_{i=1}^{n}\tilde{p}_i dx_i = 0 \tag{2.24}$$

This gives the familiar tangency solution in quantity space, given earlier.

2.4.2   Budget Shares

The logarithmic form of Shephard's lemma is also very useful, since this gives the budget shares, $w_i = p_i x_i/m$, and again links the expenditure and distance functions. This gives:

$$w_i = \frac{\partial \log E(p,U)}{\partial \log p_i} = \frac{\partial \log D(x,U)}{\partial \log x_i} \tag{2.25}$$

2.5   Price Changes and Demand Elasticities

Differentiate the Hicksian demand for good i, making use of the relationship given above between Hicksian and Marshallian demands, to give:

$$\frac{\partial x_i^H}{\partial p_j} = \frac{\partial x_i^M}{\partial m}\frac{\partial E}{\partial p_j} + \frac{\partial x_i^M}{\partial p_j} \tag{2.26}$$

so that, using Shephard's lemma:

$$\frac{\partial x_i^H}{\partial p_j} = \frac{\partial x_i^M}{\partial m}x_j + \frac{\partial x_i^M}{\partial p_j} \tag{2.27}$$

This is the famous Slutsky theorem. This can be converted into the following relationship among elasticities:

$$\sigma_{ij} = w_j e_i + \eta_{ij} \tag{2.28}$$

where e_i is the income (total expenditure) elasticity:

$$e_i = \frac{\partial x_i^M}{\partial m} \frac{m}{x_i} \tag{2.29}$$

η_{ij} is the Marshallian price elasticity of demand for good i, for a change in the price of good j, and is given by:

$$\eta_{ij} = \frac{\partial x_i^M / x_i^M}{\partial p_j / p_j} = \frac{\partial x_i^M}{\partial p_j} \frac{p_j}{x_i^M} \tag{2.30}$$

and σ_{ij} is the corresponding compensated elasticity relating to movements along a Hicksian demand curve, given by:

$$\sigma_{ij} = \frac{\partial x_i^H}{\partial p_j} \frac{p_j}{x_i^H} \tag{2.31}$$

From Shephard's lemma, $x_i^H = \partial E(p, U) / \partial p_i$, so the compensated elasticities can be written as:

$$\sigma_{ij} = \frac{\partial^2 E(p, U)}{\partial p_i \partial p_j} \frac{p_j}{x_i^H} \tag{2.32}$$

The matrix of compensated elasticities is therefore not symmetric. However, the substitution elasticities, s_{ij}, are defined as $s_{ij} = \sigma_{ij}/w_j$, and these are symmetric, in view of the symmetry of the $\partial^2 E(p, U) / \partial p_i \partial p_j$.

Other restrictions on elasticities arise from the budget constraint, giving the results that $\sum_{i=1}^{n} w_i = 1$, $\sum_{i=1}^{n} w_i e_i = 1$. The condition that $\sum_{j=1}^{n} \eta_{ij} = -e_i$ arises from the fact that the demand functions are homogeneous of degree zero, so that Euler's law gives $\sum_{j=1}^{n} (\partial x_i / \partial p_j) \, dp_j + (\partial x_i / \partial m) \, dm = 0$. In addition, the homogeneity conditions give $\sum_{j=1}^{n} w_j \sigma_{ij} = 0$ and $\sum_{j=1}^{n} s_{ij} = 0$.

The matrix $\left[\frac{\partial^2 E(p,U)}{\partial p_i \partial p_j} \right]$ is known as the Slutsky matrix, while the symmetric matrix $\left[\frac{\partial^2 D(x,U)}{\partial x_i \partial x_j} \right]$ is known as the Antonelli matrix.

2.6 Aggregation Over Consumers

The above analysis has considered only a single consumer. But the question arises of whether it is possible to aggregate over consumers, such that aggregate consumption can be expressed as a function of aggregate income and the aggregate function looks just like the individuals' functions. For this to be possible, an immediate requirement is that aggregate demand must not be affected by a change in the distribution of income, with the total income unchanged. If a change in income distribution is not to affect the total consumption of a good, then the changes arising from income gains must exactly off-set changes arising from income losses of individuals. Hence the demand functions must at least be linear, with each individual having the same marginal propensity to consume. This is satisfied for identical homothetic preferences, which imply linear demand curves having the same slope through the origin for each individual. However, this restriction is extremely strong.

2.6.1 Quasi-homothetic Preferences

Consider the following special form of indirect utility function, given by:

$$V(p, m) = a(p) + b(p) m \qquad (2.33)$$

where $a(p)$ and $b(p)$ are functions of the prices. This extends the homothetic form through the addition of the term $a(p)$, and is also known as the Gorman form. This could just as well have been written in terms of the expenditure function, the inverse of the indirect utility function, by expressing $E(p, U)$ as a linear function of U, with slope and intercept depending on prices. In this case, the intercept can then be interpreted as the cost of subsistence.

The application of Roy's identity gives the Marshallian demands:

$$x_i^M(p, m) = \alpha_i(p) + \beta_i(p) m \qquad (2.34)$$

where:

$$\alpha_i\left(p\right) = -\frac{\partial a\left(p\right)/\partial p_i}{b\left(p\right)} \tag{2.35}$$

and:

$$\beta_i\left(p\right) = -\frac{\partial b\left(p\right)/\partial p_i}{b\left(p\right)} \tag{2.36}$$

Hence the Engel curves are straight lines but, unlike the homothetic case, are not required to go through the origin.

Suppose that there are T consumers, each with Gorman indirect utility functions where the $a\left(p\right)$ can vary but the $b\left(p\right)$ are the same for each individual. The latter requirement arises because, as suggested above, exact aggregation requires that the marginal propensities of all individuals must be the same. Variations in the $a\left(p\right)$ can arise because of demographic differences, such as household composition effects. The consumption of the ith good by the jth person can be expressed as:

$$x_{i,j}^M\left(p,m_j\right) = \alpha_{i,j}\left(p\right) + \beta_i\left(p\right)m_j \tag{2.37}$$

and aggregate consumption is:

$$\sum_{j=1}^{T} x_{i,j}^M\left(p,m_j\right) = \sum_{j=1}^{T}\alpha_{i,j}\left(p\right) + \beta_i\left(p\right)\sum_{j=1}^{T}m_j \tag{2.38}$$

These total demands could therefore be generated by a 'representative consumer', with income, $Y = \sum_{j=1}^{T}m_j$, equal to aggregate income and with the indirect utility function:

$$V\left(p,Y\right) = \sum_{j=1}^{T}a_j\left(p\right) + b\left(p\right)Y \tag{2.39}$$

The Gorman form is in fact both necessary and sufficient for such exact aggregation to be possible. However, less restrictive conditions are needed if the nature of the aggregation requirement is relaxed.

2.7 Conclusions

This chapter has provided a brief review of some of the results in demand analysis that are useful for welfare measurement. There are four types of demand function. These include the pair of Marshallian ordinary and inverse demand curves, and the associated pair of compensated or Hicksian demand and inverse demand curves. In each case the demand curve is associated with a constrained optimisation problem, yet it is possible to avoid the difficulties of working with first-order conditions based on Lagrangians by making use of duality results. Demand analysis necessarily plays a central role in the theory and measurement of welfare changes. Later chapters therefore make use of many of these results.

Chapter 3

Concepts of Welfare Change

The aim of studies of the welfare change imposed by price changes is to provide a money measure of an individual's change in welfare. In public finance contexts the price changes arise from the imposition of commodity and income taxes. This gives rise to the concept of the excess burden resulting from taxation, reflecting the excess of the money measure of welfare change over the tax revenue, in well-specified situations.

The subject of welfare changes is in many ways central to microeconomic theory and their measurement involves all the complexities of applied demand analysis; the related literature is therefore vast. This chapter provides an introduction to various measures of welfare change, paying particular attention to the measurement issues involved. It does not pretend to be an exhaustive survey of the huge number of contributions to this broad topic, but attempts to pull some of the threads of the literature together. For a discussion of issues, concentrating on theoretical issues of consumer surplus, see Becht (1995). Broad-ranging treatments include McKenzie (1983), Auerbach (1985) and Johansson (1987). For studies concentrating more on measurement aspects, see Blundell *et al.* (1994).

A brief glance at the literature reveals two major features. First, the subject has been characterised by a great deal of logomachy, with consequent confusion over some of the terminology. Secondly, despite the fact that the topic provides a prime example of a 'meeting place' between theory and applications which is reflected in its major contributions, there has been a strong dichotomy between theoretical and empirical studies. Few of those proposing theoretical advances have attempted to make empirical estimates while few of those producing numerical estimates have made use of the latest theoretical advances. This and the following chapter attempt to clarify the major concepts, while placing much emphasis on practical measurement issues.

Section 3.1 begins by summarising the definitions of welfare change, in particular the compensating and equivalent variations, comparing these with the famous Marshallian measure of consumer surplus. Section 3.2 presents measures of the excess burden arising from taxation that are associated with the different welfare change measures.

The standard money measures of welfare change and excess burden involve the expenditure function, defined as the minimum cost of reaching a specified indifference curve for a given a set of prices. The relevant demand concept is therefore usually that of Hicksian, or compensated, demand curves rather than the Marshallian demand curves which are sometimes very misleadingly said to be directly observable. The problem immediately arises that calculation of the welfare measures appears at first sight to require knowledge of the precise form of utility, and hence expenditure, functions. Several responses to this problem have been adopted. One approach is to use an approximation to the true measure which involves compensated demand elasticities but does not depend on the form of utility functions; this type of approximation is also examined in section 3.2. The overall evaluation of tax changes can then be carried out in terms of aggregate values of money welfare changes.

An alternative approach in which the overall evaluation of changes is based on the specification of a social welfare function defined in terms of individuals' utilities, and explicitly allowing for aversion to inequality on the part of the judge, is discussed in section 3.3. In this case, approximations depend on the values of Marshallian, rather than compensated, demand changes. The analysis of marginal tax reform using such social welfare functions also requires substantially less information, and this is also examined in section 3.3.

Section 3.4 discusses excess burdens in the special context of income taxation and labour supply variations. This context raises no new fundamental issues, but warrants special attention given the importance of income taxation, and the fact that a change in the net wage rate, the price of leisure, has a more complex effect than a change in a typical commodity price.

The treatment of income taxation leads to the subject of the marginal welfare cost of taxation and of public funds, which is examined in section 3.4. The excess burden measures are essentially concerned with comparisons of a distortionary tax system with a non-distortionary system, that is lump sum taxation, which is assumed to raise the same revenue. However, increases in taxation from an existing tax-distorted situation are often required in order to raise additional revenue which is used to finance public expenditure. Analysis of this type of balanced budget operation is similar to the excess burden calculation only if the additional public expenditure is equivalent to a cash transfer. Otherwise the expenditure can have important implications for the yield of existing taxes. This also means that, starting from a tax-distorted system, lump sum taxes can affect the ability of existing taxes to collect revenue. This type of consideration leads to the important concept of the 'marginal cost of funds', which is also discussed in section 3.4

3.1 Defining Welfare Changes

The aim is to define a money measure of the change in welfare, experienced by a single individual, that results from a change in prices. Such a measure is provided by the change in the cost of reaching a specified indifference curve. This is appropriate because any monotonic transformation of the individual's utility function involves only a change in the (arbitrary) utility level attached to the indifference curves; it does not produce a change in the cost of reaching the curves. As in chapter 2, reference is often made to the concept of a 'money metric' utility measure, which is a particular normalisation of the utility function (although the term is sometimes used quite loosely). For more detailed discussion of money metrics, see McKenzie (1983) and Blackorby and Donaldson (1988).

A fundamental ingredient in the construction of measures of welfare change is the concept of the expenditure function, $E\left(p,U\right)$, which gives the minimum cost of achieving the utility level U for the set of prices denoted by the vector $p = (p_1, ..., p_n)$. For a discussion of its uses in public finance, see Diamond and McFadden (1974). Suppose that prices and utility are initially U^0 and p^0. Then prices change to p^1 which, after the associated change in consumption, results in a new utility level of U^1. The two major measures are defined in the next subsection.

3.1.1   Compensating and Equivalent Variations

The compensating variation, CV, is the amount of money that must be given to a loser, or taken from a gainer, in order to keep the individual on the initial indifference curve. In terms of the expenditure function, it can be written as:

$$CV = E\left(p^1, U^0\right) - E\left(p^0, U^0\right) \tag{3.1}$$

The term $E\left(p^0, U^0\right)$ is the total expenditure level in the initial situation, denoted by m^0.

The equivalent variation, EV, is defined as:

$$EV = E\left(p^1, U^1\right) - E\left(p^0, U^1\right) \tag{3.2}$$

and is therefore the amount that the individual would be prepared to pay, in the new situation, to avoid the price change. The term $E\left(p^1, U^1\right)$ is the total expenditure after the price change, denoted by m^1. The equivalent variation for a change from p^0 to p^1 is thus equal to the (negative of the) compensating variation for a change from p^1 to p^0. McKenzie (1983, p.37) prefered to think of this as another way of defining the equivalent variation, rather than an 'equivalence', in view of his objections to the compensating variation.

These welfare changes are associated with the standard decomposition of the effect of a price change into a substitution and an income effect. If $V(p,m)$ denotes the indirect utility function, then the compensating and

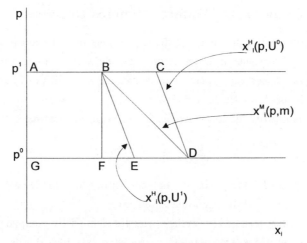

Figure 3.1: Compensating and Equivalent Variations

equivalent variations are defined implicitly by $V\left(p^1, m^0 + CV\right) = V\left(p^0, m^0\right)$ and $V\left(p^0, m^1 - EV\right) = V\left(p^1, m^1\right)$.

Consider the case of a change in the price of a single good, good i, illustrated in Figure 3.1, with $m^0 = m^1$ and incomes deflated by using the price of the other goods. The points B and D show the price and consumption levels associated with, respectively, the pre- and post-change prices. The points C and E show the price and consumption levels associated with the unobserved tangency positions on, respectively, the initial indifference curve with the new prices (so that U^0 is fixed) and the new indifference curve with the old prices (so that U^1 is fixed). Hence B and D are two observed positions on the Marshallian demand curve, denoted $x_i^M\left(p, m\right)$, while B and E are two positions on the Hicksian demand curve (or compensated demand curve) for utility constant at U^1, denoted $x_i^H(p, U^1)$. Similarly, points C and D are two unobserved points along the Hicksian demand curve for utility constant at U^0, denoted $x_i^H(p, U^0)$.

3.1.2   Converting Welfare Changes to Areas

The diagrammatic equivalents of the expressions in (3.1) and (3.2) are not
immediately apparent. In order to describe the welfare changes in terms of
the diagram a method is needed of converting expenditure functions into
Hicksian demand functions. This is achieved by using an important property
of the expenditure function whereby, from Shephard's lemma:

$$x_i^H (p, U) = \frac{\partial E (p, U)}{\partial p_i}$$ (3.3)

By integrating (3.3), the value of the expenditure function for a given price,
say p_i^1, can therefore be regarded as an area, $\int_0^{p_i^1} x_i^H (p, U) \, dp_i$, for the appropriate utility level. The welfare changes defined by compensating and
equivalent variations are therefore represented by areas to the left of the
Hicksian demand curves, between prices p_i^0 and p_i^1, for U^0 and U^1 respectively; CV is the area $ACDG$, while EV is the area $ABEG$. For example,
the equivalent variation is expressed as:

$$EV = \int_{p_i^0}^{p_i^1} x_i^H \left(p, U^1 \right) dp_i = \int_{p_i^0}^{p_i^1} \frac{\partial E (p, U^1)}{\partial p_i} dp_i$$ (3.4)

In the case of many price changes, the welfare changes resulting from the
set of price changes, where the price vector changes from p^0 to p^1, can be
written:

$$CV = \sum_{i=1}^{n} \int_{p_i^0}^{p_i^1} x_i^H \left(p, U^0 \right) dp_i$$ (3.5)

$$EV = \sum_{i=1}^{n} \int_{p_i^0}^{p_i^1} x_i^H \left(p, U^1 \right) dp_i$$ (3.6)

The famous measure of the change in consumer's surplus associated with
Marshall (1961) is, in the case of a single price change, the area $ABDG$ in
Figure 3.1. It can be seen that the Marshallian measure of welfare change
lies between the compensating and equivalent variations. For this reason, it
is often argued that it provides a reasonable approximation where changes
in a single market are being considered. The use of the Marshallian measure as an approximation has been considered by, among others, Foster and

Neuburger (1974) and Willig (1976). However, it is known that very strong and unrealistic assumptions are required for consumer's surplus to be a theoretically satisfactory measure of welfare change resulting from price changes; for a detailed statement of the conditions, see Chipman and Moore (1980).

In the case of more than one price change, the consumer's surplus measure is not well defined because its magnitude depends on the order in which the terms are evaluated in the surplus expression given by $\sum_{i=1}^{n} \int_{p_i^0}^{p_i^1} x_i^M(p,m)\, dp_i$. This is the 'path dependency problem'; see Dahlby (1977) and the references cited therein. Stahl (1985) has attempted to overcome this problem using the concept of a 'monotonic variation', defined as the Marshall integral over an operationally defined 'monotonic path'.

3.1.3 Quantity Changes

The emphasis of this chapter is on price changes associated with tax changes, but it is perhaps useful briefly to indicate how welfare changes associated with quantity changes can be defined. These are required in contexts in which it is not appropriate to regard the quantity as the dependent variable. The appropriate concept is that of the inverse demand function, $p_i(x,m)$, where the price is expressed as a function of the budget and the vector of quantities; see chapter 2 for further details.

The welfare measures for a change in a single quantity can be expressed in terms of areas underneath the appropriate compensated inverse demand curves. The latter can be obtained from the distance function, $D(x,U)$, which represents the amount by which each element of x must be scaled (divided) in order to get on to the indifference curve associated with the utility level, U. The distance function is in fact the dual corresponding to the expenditure function, and is obtained from the direct utility function by inversion, just as the expenditure function is obtained from the indirect utility function by inversion; see, for example, Deaton (1979). Shephard's lemma applied to the distance function gives:

$$\tilde{p}_i^H = \frac{\partial D(x,U)}{\partial x_i} \tag{3.7}$$

where $\tilde{p}_i$ is the normalised price, p_i/m, and the superscript H indicates that it is the associated Hicksian or compensated inverse demand curve. When m again remains unchanged, the welfare changes, ΔW, resulting from a change in quantities from x^0 to x^1, which gives rise to a utility change from U^0 to U^1, can be expressed as:

$$\Delta W = \sum_{i=1}^{n} \int_{x_i^0}^{x_i^1} \frac{\partial D\left(x, U^k\right)}{\partial x_i} dx_i \qquad (3.8)$$

and when k takes the values 0 and 1 respectively, (3.8) gives the compensating and equivalent variations. For further discussion of welfare changes arising from quantity changes, see Youn Kim (1997). In addition, the quantities consumed of some goods may be rationed, giving rise to further complications; see Breslaw and Smith (1995).

3.2   The Excess Burden of Taxation

The price changes that generate the welfare changes discussed above may in many contexts be regarded as resulting from the imposition of taxes. The distortions arising from taxation impose an excess burden that is in addition to the revenue collected. The burden measures the cost of not being able to impose true lump sum taxes. Alternative concepts of excess burden arise, depending on whether compensating or equivalent variations are used. The first subsection below defines excess burdens and marginal excess burdens. The second subsection considers the use of approximations which do not require the form of the utility or expenditure function to be known, needing only elasticities evaluated at current consumption levels. The final subsection considers marginal tax reform where value judgements enter explicitly, but again the informational requirements are reduced.

3.2.1   Excess Burden Concepts

First, consider the excess burden defined as the amount, in excess of taxation paid, that the individual would give up to have all taxes removed. Hence the comparison is with respect to the absence of all taxes; marginal tax changes are considered later in this section. This definition gives an excess burden, B_E, based on the equivalent variation, as follows:

$$B_E = EV - R\left(p^1, m^1\right) \tag{3.9}$$

where $R\left(p^1, m^1\right)$ is the revenue collected from the individual. The burden is sometimes defined in microeconomics texts so that it is negative for a tax increase, but the following uses the more common approach found in public finance studies. In the case of a set of taxes per unit of output, t_i, this is given by:

$$R\left(p^1, m^1\right) = \sum_{i=1}^{n} t_i x_i^M\left(p_i^1, m^1\right) \tag{3.10}$$

Alternatively, the excess burden may be defined in terms of the amount, in addition to the revenue collected from the individual, that would need to be returned in order to keep utility at the pre-tax level. This gives a burden, B_C, based on the compensating variation, as follows:

$$B_C = CV - R\left(p^1, E\left(p^1, U^0\right)\right) \tag{3.11}$$

The excess burden associated with the compensating variation is, however, sometimes defined simply by subtracting the actual revenue, as defined in (3.10). The definitions given here follow those given by Auerbach (1985). The revenue subtracted from the CV is higher than in (3.10) because of the tax arising from the compensation involved in order to maintain utility at U^0. The value of R can be expressed using the relationship between the Marshallian and Hicksian demand curves such that, in general:

$$x^M\left(p, m\right) = x^M\left(p, E\left(p, U\right)\right) = x^H\left(p, U\right) \tag{3.12}$$

Movement in the other direction involves the relation:

$$x^H\left(p, U\right) = x^H\left(p, V\left(p, m\right)\right) = x^M\left(p, m\right) \tag{3.13}$$

where V denotes the indirect utility function. Hence, the revenue in equation (3.11) can be written as:

$$R\left(p^1, E\left(p^1, U^0\right)\right) = \sum_{i=1}^{n} t_i x_i^H \left(p_i^1, U^0\right) \tag{3.14}$$

One immediate implication of the above measures is that, because of the relevance of the Hicksian demands in obtaining the EV and CV, there may be a substantial excess burden with a single tax even when the good in question has a zero own-price elasticity of demand.

The above discussion refers to the burden of taxation compared with the absence of taxes. Consider an increase in taxation, such that each tax rate increases by Δt_i, to $t_i + \Delta t_i$ per unit, and prices increase from p^1 to p^2. The marginal excess burden, ΔB_E, associated with the equivalent variation resulting from such a tax increase is the amount that the consumer would pay, in addition to the extra tax, in order to avoid the increase. Hence:

$$\Delta B_E = m^2 - E\left(p^1, U^2\right) - \left\{R\left(p^2, m^2\right) - R\left(p^1, m^2\right)\right\} \tag{3.15}$$

It is important to recognise that the change in revenue on the right-hand side of (3.15) cannot simply be expressed, for each good, as the change in the tax rate, Δt_i, multiplied by the new quantity demanded. This is because the extra tax means that the consumption of each good falls further; this in turn means that the revenue associated with the initial tax rate of t_i falls correspondingly. This type of argument has important implications for measures of the marginal welfare cost of taxation discussed below.

Using the above approach, equation (3.15) can be rearranged to give:

$$\begin{aligned}
\Delta B_E &= m^2 - E\left(p^1, U^2\right) - \sum_{i=1}^{n} \Delta t_i x_i^M \left(p_i^2, m^2\right) \\
&\quad + \sum_{i=1}^{n} t_i \left\{x_i^H \left(p_i^1, U^2\right) - x_i^M \left(p_i^2, m^2\right)\right\}
\end{aligned} \tag{3.16}$$

The tax revenue measures above are all given for a tax per unit of output, but it is often necessary to consider *ad valorem* taxes in which the tax rate is expressed as a proportion of the value of each good. Suppose that t_i now denotes the tax-exclusive rate imposed on good i. Since the prices faced by consumers are tax-inclusive, the expression for total revenue must use the equivalent tax-inclusive rate, $t_i/\left(1 + t_i\right)$. Hence equation (3.10) becomes:

$$R\left(p^1, m^1\right) = \sum_{i=1}^{n} \left(\frac{t_i}{1+t_i}\right) p_i x_i^M \left(p_i^1, m^1\right) \tag{3.17}$$

The question arises of whether any particular measure of welfare change, and hence excess burden, is superior to others. Several authors, for example Kay (1980), Pazner and Sadka (1980), King (1983), McKenzie (1983) and Pauwels (1986), have argued that the equivalent variation is superior. In the case of the compensating variation the welfare loss is based on the post-tax prices, whereas the tax revenue is measured in terms of values based on the pre-tax prices. If several alternative tax policies are examined, the compensating variation has the theoretically unsatisfactory property that it gives comparisons involving different prices for each policy. These problems do not arise with the use of equivalent variations. Furthermore, the excess burden based on the equivalent variation is minimised at optimal tax rates, unlike the compensating variation. A detailed comparison of alternative excess burden measures was made by Mayshar (1990). For an axiomatic treatment of alternative welfare change measures, see Ebert (1995), who showed that no measure can claim to be unequivocally superior to others and that the choice of measure cannot avoid value judgements.

3.2.2 Approximating the Excess Burden

One very common approach to measurement difficulties, following Harberger (1964), is to give up any attempt to provide a precise measure, requiring detailed information about utility functions and associated expenditure functions, and to employ an approximation to welfare changes. For example, following the introduction of a tax structure, taking a Taylor series expansion of $E\left(p^1, U\right) - E\left(p^0, U\right)$ and neglecting higher-order terms gives:

$$E\left(p^1, U\right) - E\left(p^0, U\right) = \sum_{i=1}^{n} \frac{\partial E}{\partial p_i} dp_i + \frac{1}{2} \sum_{i=1}^{n} \sum_{j=1}^{n} \frac{\partial^2 E}{\partial p_i \partial p_j} dp_i dp_j \tag{3.18}$$

Since the tax revenue can be expressed, using $dp_i = p_i^1 - p_i^0$, as $\sum_{i=1}^{n} x_i dp_i = \sum_{i=1}^{n} \frac{\partial E}{\partial p_i} dp_i$, which is the same as the first term in (3.18), the excess burden is approximated by:

$$B = \frac{1}{2} \sum_{i=1}^{n} \sum_{j=1}^{n} s_{ij} dp_i dp_j \tag{3.19}$$

where s_{ij} is the i,jth element of the symmetric matrix S and $s_{ij} = \partial x_i^H / \partial p_j = \partial^2 E(p, U) / \partial p_i \partial p_j$. This enables the excess burden to be approximated without knowing the precise form of the utility function, so long as estimates of the compensated elasticities are available. Furthermore, for such small changes there is no distinction between the burden defined in terms of compensated and equivalent variations.

The use of such approximations makes the calculation of excess burdens relatively quick and cheap, partly because the usual approach is to obtain elasticities from other demand studies, which in turn usually means that a high level of aggregation is considered. This kind of approach gives rough illustrative calculations and sensitivity analyses are unfortunately rarely reported. A more serious use of the approximations would involve obtaining, subject to data availability, compensated demand elasticities for a range of demographic or other groups, and providing sensitivity analyses (based perhaps on the estimated standard errors of the demand function parameters).

The approximate welfare change measures may be used on the argument that, because only the first derivatives of demand functions are required, they are not likely to be very sensitive to the precise specification of the demand equations estimated. This is an important point, so long as attention is restricted to small tax changes. Critics of such an approach would argue (based on the use of methods discussed in chapter 4) that the additional cost of producing the exact welfare measures is negligible, so that at least it would be helpful to compare results.

The approach considered in this subsection is to take a second-order approximation to the excess burden for a single individual. In evaluating the overall effect of a tax change, use is often made of the aggregate value of excess burdens in a specified population group. This is equivalent to the use of a social welfare function defined as a simple sum of such burdens, so it implies no aversion to inequality on the part of the judge. An alternative approach is to specify a social welfare function which differs in two ways from the total burden. First, the welfare function may be specified in terms of individual utilities, and secondly the form of the welfare function may allow for some aversion to inequality. This approach is considered in the next section.

3.3 Social Welfare Changes

3.3.1 A Social Welfare Function

Instead of considering the aggregate value of welfare change measures, a social welfare function can be specified in terms of individual utilities. If V_h denotes the (indirect) utility of the hth household (for $h = 1, ..., H$), then the welfare function, W, can be expressed in general terms as $W = W(V_1, ..., V_H)$. The first derivative of W with respect to the price of the ith good is given by:

$$\frac{\partial W}{\partial p_i} = \sum_{h=1}^{H} \frac{\partial W}{\partial V_h} \frac{\partial V_h}{\partial p_i} \tag{3.20}$$

Use can then be made of Roy's identity, which establishes a link between the Marshallian demands and the indirect utility function, such that (omitting the M superscript for convenience):

$$x_{hi}(p, m_h) = -\frac{\partial V_h(p, m_h)/\partial p_i}{\partial V_h(p, m_h)/\partial m_h} \tag{3.21}$$

Hence:

$$\frac{\partial W}{\partial p_i} = -\sum_{h=1}^{H} v_h x_{hi} \tag{3.22}$$

with:

$$v_h = \frac{\partial W}{\partial V_h} \frac{\partial V_h}{\partial m_h} \tag{3.23}$$

The term v_h can be interpreted as the social marginal utility of income of household h. The vs therefore define a set of distributional weights. These weights are in general not independent of prices; for a statement of the conditions on both welfare and utility functions required for independence, see

Banks *et al.* (1996, pp.1230-1232). Differentiation of (3.22) with respect to p_i gives the second derivative:

$$\frac{\partial^2 W}{\partial p_i^2} = -\sum_{h=1}^{H} \left(\frac{\partial v_h}{\partial p_i} x_{hi} + \frac{\partial x_{hi}}{\partial p_i} v_h \right) \tag{3.24}$$

3.3.2 Approximating Social Welfare Changes

The above results can be used to obtain a second-order approximation to a change in social welfare, ΔW, resulting from a change in the price of the ith good of Δp_i. The Taylor expansion, ignoring third and higher-order terms, gives:

$$\frac{\Delta W}{\Delta p_i} \approx \frac{\partial W}{\partial p_i} + \frac{\Delta p_i}{2} \frac{\partial^2 W}{\partial p_i^2} \tag{3.25}$$

Substitution for the first and second derivatives, using (3.22) and (3.24) gives, as in Banks *et al.* (1996, p.1229):

$$\frac{\Delta W}{\Delta p_i} = -\sum_{h=1}^{H} v_h x_{hi} \left[1 + \frac{\Delta p_i}{2p_i} \left(\frac{\partial \log v_h}{\partial \log p_i} + \frac{\partial \log x_{hi}}{\partial \log p_i} \right) \right] \tag{3.26}$$

The first point to note about this second-order approximation is that it involves the use of Marshallian own-price demand elasticities, whereas the approximation using the excess burden measure involves the use of compensated demand elasticities.

A special case of this approximation is of interest. Suppose that there is no aversion to inequality, so $v_h = 1$ for all h. The change in social welfare becomes, on substituting (7.3) and (3.24) into (3.25):

$$\Delta W = -\Delta p_i \left\{ \sum_{h=1}^{H} x_{hi} + \frac{\Delta p_i}{2} \frac{\partial \sum_{h=1}^{H} x_{hi}}{\partial p_i} \right\} \tag{3.27}$$

The first implication of equal welfare weights is that only the aggregate quantity change is relevant. If the price change arises from the introduction of a tax per unit of $t_i = \Delta p_i$, then the first term in (3.27), $-\Delta p_i \sum_{h=1}^{H} x_{hi}$, is the total tax revenue arising from this good, based on the pre-tax total quantity. If taxes are already imposed on other goods, then the aggregate tax revenue must allow for substitution effects. This is treated in the following subsection. Subtracting this from the absolute value of the welfare change, and writing $\partial \sum_{h=1}^{H} x_{hi}/\partial p_i$ as $\Delta \sum_{h=1}^{H} x_{hi}/\Delta p_i$, gives the approximation to the excess welfare burden, B_W, of:

$$B_W = \frac{t_i}{2} \Delta \sum_{h=1}^{H} x_{hi} \tag{3.28}$$

Hence, in the case where a new tax is imposed on a single good, the second-order approximation to the social welfare loss, in excess of the tax revenue, is simply half the tax rate multiplied by the change in the aggregate quantity consumed. This is of course the famous measure, based on the area of a triangle associated with the market demand curve, that was produced by Dupuit (1844) and Jenkin (1871). It continues to be presented in the vast majority of introductory text books, motivated simply by the use of the standard Marshallian consumer and producer surplus concepts applied to market curves.

It was mentioned earlier, when discussing Figure 3.1, that for a single price change the change in Marshallian consumer surplus lies between the compensating and equivalent variations, so that in some cases the Marshallian measure may provide a reasonable approximation to a theoretically more appealing measure. However, the same cannot be said of the corresponding excess burden, which can differ substantially from the exact measure.

The use of first- and second-order approximations, using social welfare functions based on both money welfare changes and utility for each household, and allowing for different degrees of aversion to inequality, has been examined by Banks *et al.* (1996). They found (in the context of the elimination of exemptions for value added taxation) that second-order approximations do indeed perform quite well in terms of welfare changes, but they did not report excess burdens. Obviously, the approximations perform better the smaller is the price change examined.

3.3.3   Marginal Tax Reform

One approach is to concentrate exclusively on small, or marginal, tax changes. Using the above social welfare function, specified in terms of utilities, the marginal change in social welfare resulting from a change in the price of the ith good is given simply by the expression for $\partial W/\partial p_i$ given in equation (3.22) above. The method, pioneered by Feldstein (1972) and extended by Ahmad and Stern (1984), involves comparing, for each commodity, the marginal change in social welfare arising from a tax change with the marginal change in total tax revenue. The change in aggregate tax revenue arising from a marginal change in any single tax must now allow for the consequent changes in taxation arising from existing taxes on all other goods, because of substitution effects.

If, as before, t_i is the tax per unit imposed on good i, then aggregate tax revenue, R, is given by:

$$R = \sum_{h=1}^{H} \sum_{k=1}^{n} t_k x_{hk} \tag{3.29}$$

Differentiating with respect to the ith tax rate, and using $\partial p_i = \partial t_i$, on the assumption that the tax is fully passed on to consumers, gives:

$$\frac{\partial R}{\partial t_i} = \sum_{h=1}^{H} x_{hi} + \sum_{h=1}^{H} \sum_{k=1}^{n} t_k \frac{\partial x_{hk}}{\partial p_i} \tag{3.30}$$

The ratio $(\partial W/\partial t_i)\,/\,(\partial R/\partial t_i) = 1/\rho_i$ measures the change in social welfare per dollar of extra tax revenue resulting from a marginal change in the tax. In order to avoid a discontinuity if the change in revenue is zero, Madden (1995) suggested taking the value of ρ_i, giving the marginal revenue cost of reform. For an optimal tax system, the marginal revenue cost of reform must be equal for all goods. Hence, the *direction* of a marginal tax reform is indicated by the relative magnitudes of this ratio for each commodity group. Furthermore, by multiplying numerator and denominator by p_i, an expression involving expenditures (rather than quantities) and cross-price elasticities is obtained. In particular, the change in revenue is $p_i X_i + \sum_k \tau_k \eta_{ki} p_k X_k$, where X_i is aggregate demand, η_{ki} is the elasticity of demand for k with respect to the price of i, and τ_k is the ratio of the tax to the tax-inclusive price.

The method can be used for alternative specifications of the social welfare function, giving rise to alternative sets of the v_hs. In practice, it is usual to specify the social welfare function in terms of each household's total expenditure (adjusted using equivalent household scales), rather than utility. The conditions under which this is consistent are given by Banks *et al.* (1996, p.1232). It does not imply price-independence.

This approach requires expenditure data to be available for each commodity group at the household level, but a useful property of (3.30) is that it involves only aggregate Marshallian changes in demand, evaluated at the current position. This gives a considerable reduction in information required. The approach was initially used by Ahmad and Stern (1984) in the context of a developing country where data are relatively scarce, but it has since been used in developed countries; for applications and further references see Newbery and Stern (1987), Newbery (1995), Mayshar and Yitzhaki (1995), and Madden (1995, 1996, 1997). Deaton and Ng (1996) considered both parametric and non-parametric methods of obtaining the demand changes.

The problems of obtaining the aggregate elasticities should not of course be neglected. Comparisons of the implications of using alternative demand systems, carried out by Madden (1996), showed that similar results are obtained for different systems. This, as noted earlier, is likely in view of the fact that only demand changes at observed consumption levels are needed. He also found that the results are more sensitive to the dynamic specification of demand functions used. One practical problem is that the commodity groups which are relevant for tax purposes are not usually the same as those for which demand information is available.

3.4 Income Taxation and Labour Supply

The definitions of welfare change and excess burden given in the previous sections were discussed in the context of commodity taxes. The application of the concepts of welfare change and excess burden to the analysis of income taxation requires no new principles, but involves some subtle differences that are worth discussing. The compensating and equivalent variations resulting from an income tax change are examined in the first subsection. The special problems arising from the existence of nonlinear budget constraints are discussed in the second subsection. The third subsection considers general equilibrium implications. Finally, approximations to excess burdens in the context of income taxation are presented.

The demand model can easily be extended, following the standard method of adding the consumption of leisure to the utility function and modifying the budget constraint accordingly. On tax and transfer systems with labour supply responses, and further references to the literature, see Creedy (1994, 1996). One effect of an income tax is that it affects the price of leisure, or its opportunity cost in terms of the consumption of goods. The standard demand model involves maximisation of a utility function $U(x)$ subject to a budget constraint $m = \sum_{i=1}^{n} p_i x_i$, where x_i and p_i are consumption and tax-inclusive prices respectively. When the proportion of time devoted to leisure, h, is added, then the utility function becomes $U(x, h)$ and the budget constraint is changed to:

$$w(1 - h) + g = \sum_{i=1}^{n} p_i x_i \qquad (3.31)$$

where g represents non-wage income and w is the net-of-tax wage rate. In some contexts, g may be influenced by a transfer system and may also depend on t. For example, if the income tax has a tax-free threshold, so that tax is a proportion of income measured in excess of the threshold, then for taxpayers this is equivalent to a proportional tax combined with a transfer payment equal to the threshold multiplied by the tax rate.

Rearrangement of (3.31) shows that this augmented model is equivalent to having an additional good, leisure, with a price of w, and a modified form of exogenous income, where m, is replaced by 'full income', M, and:

$$M = w + g \qquad (3.32)$$

Full income is therefore the value of earnings that would be obtained if all available time were spent working (that is, if $h = 0$), plus any non-wage income, g. The expenditure function in this context gives the minimum full income needed to achieve a given utility level at a specified wage and set of goods prices. A reduction in the net wage rate, resulting from an increase in income taxation, directly reduces the price of leisure and, through (3.32), involves a drop in the value of full income by reducing the market value of the individual's endowment of time. It is this dual effect that complicates the effect on welfare of an income tax change.

There is not unanimity with regard to treatment of the expenditure function in this case. Some authors, for example Walker (1993, p.34-36), define the expenditure function as giving the minimum non-wage income, rather than full income. In the standard indifference curve diagram of labour/leisure choice, the welfare change measures can conveniently be shown in terms of changes in non-wage income. However, the present approach is preferred partly because it reflects the minimum cost of consuming all goods, including leisure. It can also be adopted without modification to deal with tax changes in general equilibrium, where pre-tax factor prices also change.

3.4.1 Compensating and Equivalent Variations

The expressions for the compensating and equivalent variations, given earlier, need to be modified slightly in order to allow for the fact that full income and the price of leisure change in opposite directions when the income tax structure changes. The net-of-tax wage rate falls from w^0 to w^1 as a result of an income tax.

First, consider the compensating variation. The amount that an individual would need to be given to compensate for an increase in income taxation is equal to the full income that, at the new prices, would enable the old utility level to be reached, $E\left(w^1, U^0\right)$, less the full income obtained under the higher tax, M^1. Hence $CV = E\left(w^1, U^0\right) - M^1$. The former measure, the full income needed for U^0 at post tax wage w^1 is, in the case of an income tax increase, less than the original full income. This is because the tax increase involves a reduction in the price of a good, in this case leisure. The full income after the tax increase, M^1, is nevertheless below the amount needed to reach the appropriate point on the compensated leisure demand curve. If the standard definition of the compensating variation, in (3.1), is used along with expenditure functions defined in terms of non-wage income (rather than full income), the absolute value is precisely the same as the expression given in this paragraph. The same applies to the equivalent variation.

Secondly, consider the equivalent variation. The amount that the individual would be prepared to pay in the new situation in order to avoid the tax change is equal to the initial full income, M^0, less the full income that, with the initial net wage, generates the utility reached after the tax increase, $U(w^0, U^1)$. Hence $EV = M^0 - U(w^0, U^1)$. Avoiding the tax change carries with it the benefit of a higher full income (because of the higher net wage rate) but this is modified by the corresponding increase in the price of leisure. In the case of an increase in the price of a single good with a fixed labour supply, the compensating variation exceeds the equivalent variation, but in the context of variable labour supply models, the ranking for income tax changes is reversed. The complication arises essentially because of the simultaneous and opposite effect on the market value of the individual's endowment of time and the price of one of the goods (leisure) consumed. The above expressions can be used to examine the excess burdens arising from redistribution. This gives rise to different changes in the non-wage incomes of individuals. In the following diagrammatic treatment, the non-wage incomes are assumed to be fixed.

The above definitions do not at first sight appear to translate into areas, as in the case of a tax on a single commodity. Some diagrammatic treatments of the burden of income tax using labour supply curves are incorrect although the correct excess burden 'triangle' is specified; see, for example, Browning (1976, p.285; 1987, p.12). Reference is often incorrectly made to areas underneath the labour supply curve. For this reason, the area is specified in some detail here. The definitions are converted into areas by a simple transformation, whereby:

$$CV = \left\{ E\left(w^1, U^0\right) - M^0 \right\} + \left\{ M^0 - M^1 \right\} \tag{3.33}$$

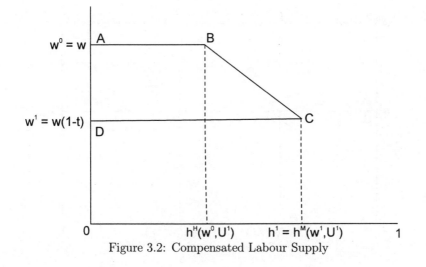

Figure 3.2: Compensated Labour Supply

$$EV = \left\{ M^1 - U\left(w^0, U^1\right) \right\} + \left\{ M^0 - M^1 \right\} \qquad (3.34)$$

The absolute value of the first term in curly brackets in each of the above expressions corresponds to an area to the left of a Hicksian (compensated) leisure demand curve between appropriate 'prices'.

The equivalent variation is shown in Figure 3.2. This shows the Hicksian demand curve for leisure which intersects the (unshown) Marshallian demand curve at $h^1 = h^M\left(w^1, M^1\right)$. The increase in welfare, the equivalent variation, arising from the reduction in the price of leisure is the area ABCD to the left of the compensated demand curve. This translates into the area, also marked ABCD, in Figure 3.3, which shows the corresponding labour supply curve; the relevant area is to the right of the supply curve. The change in full income, with no change in non-wage income, is given by the area ADGF, so that the equivalent variation is the area FBCG (equal to the area ADGF less the area ABCD). The income tax revenue, the product of labour supply and the tax per unit of labour, is given by the area FECG. Hence the equivalent variation-based excess burden of the income tax is the area ECB.

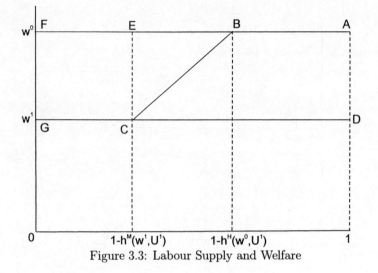

Figure 3.3: Labour Supply and Welfare

3.4.2   Nonlinear Budget Constraints

The major practical problem when extending the model to deal with labour supply and the excess burden arising from income taxation is that the income tax system is seldom proportional. Tax and transfer systems are typically nonlinear, so that in practice it is necessary to deal with piecewise linear budget constraints. For each marginal tax rate, there is a separate linear section. The tax rate faced by each individual is therefore endogenous and depends on labour supply decisions.

In calculating the welfare changes associated with a particular tax change, it is therefore necessary to check whether the individual moves to another section of the budget constraint, so that the appropriate expenditure function is used. For example, even with a proportional income tax the existence of non-wage income generates a corner solution corresponding to $h = 1$, where the individual does not work and consumes only the non-wage income. Suppose that an increase in the tax rate is just sufficient to push the individual to the corner. The equivalent variation for such a tax increase is the same as for any higher tax rise.

This point can be illustrated by the following example. Suppose the individual has Cobb-Douglas preferences $U = c^\alpha h^{1-\alpha}$, and $\alpha = 0.7$, with non-wage income, g, equal to 25. A minimum wage of $w_L = g(1 - \alpha)/\alpha = 10.714$ is required for $h < 1$. Suppose that in the absence of taxation, $w = 15$, so that the individual works and $h = 0.8$ with $c = 28$. A tax rate of $t = 0.3$ means that the net wage is 10.5 so that $h = 1$ and $c = 25$, giving $U^1 = 9.518$. The expenditure function is $U \left(\frac{1}{\alpha}\right)^\alpha \left(\frac{w}{1-\alpha}\right)^{1-\alpha}$, so the equivalent variation is $40 - 9.518 \left(\frac{1}{\alpha}\right)^\alpha \left(\frac{15}{1-\alpha}\right)^{1-\alpha}$. This is the same as for a higher t because U^1 is unaffected. Over the range where $h = 1$, the expenditure function is $U^{1/\alpha}/\alpha$, so the compensating variation is given by $\frac{1}{\alpha} \left(28^\alpha 0.8^{1-\alpha}\right)^{1/\alpha} - (10.5 + 25)$. This is higher for a higher value of t, since the net wage would be lower than 10.5.

The implication of piecewise budget constraints that are concave is that there tends to be a bunching of individuals at the corners. The use of means-testing in transfer systems means, however, that there may be convex parts of the constraint, which can generate discrete jumps at certain wage rates. On this type of phenomenon see Lambert (1985) and Creedy (1996). Furthermore, some budget constraints may not be continuous, as stressed by King (1987). Any tangency solution can be regarded as arising from an equivalent simple linear income tax with a proportional tax rate and an appropriate value of non-wage income. In econometric work, appropriate techniques have been developed to deal with such kinked budget constraints; for a survey of labour supply and taxation see, for example, Hausman (1985) and Blundell (1992).

3.4.3 General Equilibrium Effects

The previous discussion has been in the context of partial equilibrium where prices facing producers were assumed to be unchanged. However, a change in income and commodity taxes is likely to affect tax-exclusive prices, wages and profits, through general equilibrium effects. The expressions in (3.33) and (3.34) can nevertheless be applied directly to the general equilibrium context, given a model that allows for the interdependencies. Several such models have been developed, and these have helped to illustrate the way in which tax incidence can differ in the general, compared with the partial, equi-

Table 3.1: Introduction of a Wage Tax

No.	x	y	p_y	Wage	Rental	Revenue
1	0.469	0.818	0.954	0.50	0.562	0
2	0.526	0.703	0.944	0.49	0.567	0.187

librium analyses, though a practical limitation is that they usually contain few individuals. One important advantage of general equilibrium models is that they force the user to be precise about the way in which the tax revenue is used.

To give an example, consider a static two-sector model with Cobb-Douglas production functions $x = L^{0.3}K^{0.7}$ and $y = L^{0.7}K^{0.3}$, where total supply of capital services is normalised to 1 and $p_x = 1$. Suppose there are two individuals with identical preferences $U = x^{0.3}y^{0.5}h^{0.2}$, and endowments of time normalised to 1 unit, where each person holds half of the available capital. Suppose the government spends 80 per cent of tax revenue on good x and the remainder on good y (though the use of transfer payments could easily be examined in this framework). Two examples are shown in Table 3.1, corresponding to zero taxation and a proportional wage tax of 30 per cent. In this case, given the government's use of tax revenue, the introduction of the wage tax leads to an increase in the output of the capital-intensive good, x, so that the gross wage rate falls slightly, while the non-wage component of full income of each individual increases slightly. The fall in the full income of each person is equal to 0.154, while the welfare rise associated with the fall in both p_y and the price of leisure is found to be 0.053. These results are obtained by making use of the expenditure function which is given in this case by $E(p, U) = U \left(\frac{1}{0.3}\right)^{0.3} \left(\frac{p_y}{0.5}\right)^{0.5} \left(\frac{w}{0.2}\right)^{0.2}$, where w is the net wage.

The net effect, from (3.34), is an equivalent variation of 0.101. Since the tax paid by each individual is 0.093, the excess burden of the wage tax is 0.008 for each person. In a partial equilibrium framework, the pre-tax wage, the prices of both goods and the capital rental would remain unchanged, giving a higher excess burden of 0.103; the proportional difference between the use of partial and general equilibrium approaches can therefore be substantial.

In practice, the general equilibrium tax models which have been constructed are at a high level of aggregation on the household side, although some of the models contain many different production sectors. It has proved to be extremely difficult to construct general equilibrium models which also handle the type of population heterogeneity that is usually required when examining the impact of detailed tax structure changes. Hence small-scale general equilibrium models have been used to examine specific issues; for an introduction to taxation in the general equilibrium framework, see Creedy (1997b). Further references to such models are made below, and for an extensive general equilibrium treatment of welfare costs of taxation, see Diewert and Lawrence (1994).

3.4.4 The Welfare Cost of Income Taxation

Several studies have focused on measuring the excess burden, or 'welfare cost', of income taxation, using an approximation to the excess burden as the measure of welfare cost: this is the area ECB in Figure 3.3 discussed above. The studies are typically carried out at a very high level of aggregation, using a representative individual. This has the significant drawback that no attempt is made to deal with the considerable degree of heterogeneity found in practice, or to obtain econometric estimates of labour supply for different groups, allowing for the nonlinear budget constraints discussed above.

The approximation involves treating the compensated labour supply (corresponding to leisure demand) curve as linear. With a pre-tax wage of $w = w^0$ and a tax rate of t, the height of the resulting triangle is $w - (1-t)\,w = tw$, the base is the change in labour supply, ΔL, so that the area of the triangle ECB is approximated by:

$$B = \frac{1}{2}tw\Delta L \qquad (3.35)$$

The term ΔL is then replaced by $(\Delta L/\Delta w)\,tw$, using $\Delta w = tw$. If L denotes the post-tax labour supply, the compensated elasticity of labour supply with respect to the wage, η, is written as:

$$\eta = \frac{\Delta L}{\Delta w}\frac{w\,(1-t)}{L} \qquad (3.36)$$

and (3.35) becomes:

$$B = \frac{1}{2}\eta w L \left(\frac{t^2}{1-t} \right) \tag{3.37}$$

Harberger (1964) and Browning (1976) initially evaluated the elasticity and earnings at pre-tax levels, giving a different value of L and omitting the term $(1-t)$ from the denominator. The correct approximation for the equivalent variation-based burden was given by Findlay and Jones (1982).

In obtaining numerical values, emphasis is usually placed on the appropriate values to use for each of the terms in (3.37), particularly t and η. The value of t is often based on an average of tax rates. The resulting welfare cost measures are sensitive to these parameters.

This kind of welfare cost measure can be obtained with relatively little cost, but the practical application of this type of approximation is severely limited. The value of such aggregative measures is called into question, given the wide dispersion within the population, the lack of a clear link in practice between the value of t used in evaluating (3.37) and the tax rates that are the focus of policy debate, and the use of aggregate elasticities which ignore the important role of corner solutions. The approximation may have some pedagogic value in helping to illustrate the factors influencing the excess burden of income taxation, but aggregate measures bear no relation to practical tax structure changes that may realistically be considered. However, the use of a very high level of aggregation is not a necessary feature of studies using this approximation. For example, Wallace and Wasylenko (1992) used Browning's approach to examine the welfare effects of the 1986 tax reforms in the US. They used elasticities based on averages quoted from other studies, but applied them to individuals in micro-data sets, grouping the results into income deciles.

3.5   Marginal Welfare Cost and Cost of Funds

The previous discussion of excess burdens and marginal excess burdens in section 3.2 was in terms of replacing, or partially replacing, a distorting tax with a lump sum tax involving no distortions. But this may not always be the relevant concept to examine, particularly where it is required to use an increase in tax revenue in order to finance an increase in government expenditure. The present section concentrates on the issues arising from this distinction. The clarification of these issues actually arose from attempts to explain the substantial differences between marginal welfare cost calculations obtained by several different authors. Browning (1987) argued that these differences arose not because of the different models (for example, partial and general equilibrium) or basic welfare concepts used, but because of the sensitivity of results to small differences in the various parameters. However, Ballard (1990) and Fullerton (1991) argued that the substantial reported differences arose also from the use of different concepts. Clarification of the marginal welfare cost concept then leads to the concept of the marginal cost of funds.

An extension of the model to allow for involuntary unemployment and sticky wages was made by Freebairn (1995), who compared results using alternative models and found wide variations. His argument is that introducing these considerations shifts the emphasis of policy discussions away from the marginal tax rate. Browning's approach was applied to New Zealand by McKeown and Woodfield (1995), who used a somewhat more disaggregated approach.

3.5.1 The Marginal Welfare Cost

In defining his marginal welfare cost of taxation measure, Browning (1987) used the difference between the equivalent variation resulting from the tax change and the change in tax revenue along the compensated demand curve, divided by the actual tax revenue after the tax change. Stuart (1984) used the difference between the compensating variation and the change in revenue, divided by the change in revenue. Alternatively, Ballard *et al.* (1985) used the difference between the equivalent variation and the change in revenue, divided by the change in revenue. Fullerton (1991) showed, for a variety of models and parameters, that the Stuart (1984) and Ballard *et al.* (1985)

measures are generally close together, but the Browning measure is typically substantially higher. The first result is not surprising, since for a truly marginal change the equivalent and compensating variations are equal.

Ballard (1990) argued that a basic distinction needs to be drawn, following Musgrave's (1959) terminology, between differential incidence and balanced-budget analyses. In the former, comparisons are made involving the same amount of government expenditure; for example, comparisons may be made between lump sum taxation and distortionary taxes used to raise the same required revenue. This is precisely the type of comparison used when defining excess burdens. In balanced-budget analyses, government expenditure is increased and at the same time the tax system is changed in order to raise the extra revenue. This is the relevant type of analysis when the finance of a government project is being considered. In a general equilibrium analysis where an increase in taxation is used to finance higher transfer payments, the balanced budget analysis is equivalent to the differential study, since there is no change in the net tax paid. However, in most applications the distinction is important.

It seems useful, following Ballard (1990), to reserve the term 'marginal welfare cost' to refer only to balanced-budget analyses, using the same concept as in Ballard *et al.* (1985) mentioned above. By contrast, the 'marginal excess burden' refers to the change in welfare divided by the amount of distortionary tax revenue replaced by a lump sum tax.

The additional government expenditure involved in a balanced budget study means that, in addition to the distortionary effects of taxation considered in the differential incidence studies of excess burden, there are income effects which need to be considered. This type of argument led Atkinson and Stern (1974) to modify the standard optimality condition for a public good, in terms of equality between the marginal rate of transformation and the sum of marginal rates of substitution between the public good and private goods. The additional tax has implications for the ability of existing taxes to raise revenue. An interesting case arises if the supply of labour is backward bending, where it is possible for the marginal welfare cost to fall when income tax is increased. Ballard and Fullerton (1992, p.125) also gave an example of additional tax revenue being used to finance a road which may give rise to an increase in the consumption of fuel. This has the effect of increasing the revenue from the existing fuel tax, irrespective of how the project is financed. These issues were also emphasised in a related paper by Triest (1990), who was concerned with the welfare cost of additional government expenditure financed from higher taxes, in a cost-benefit analyses.

These examples show that the effects of the particular new public project on behaviour, especially regarding strong complements and substitutes, need to be considered. In the case of labour supply, the public project financed from the extra taxation may have significant effects depending on complementarity or substitutability with leisure. This was stressed by Snow and Warren (1996) who, allowing for this and other effects, carried out a comprehensive comparison of alternative measures of marginal welfare costs for small tax changes. They were able to show precisely why the various estimates given in the literature differ. They argued that further progress requires the inclusion of government spending as an explanatory variable in econometric studies of labour supply. Some empirical support for the inclusion of government spending in labour supply has been provided by Conway (1997).

3.5.2 The Marginal Cost of Funds

An important implication arising from these various studies is that while the marginal excess burden, or marginal welfare cost, is relevant for differential-incidence studies, the appropriate concept when considering the finance of a public project is the marginal cost of funds, MCF. This is defined as the change in the equivalent variation divided by the change in revenue, so that:

$$MCF = \frac{\Delta(EV)}{\Delta R} \tag{3.38}$$

The marginal welfare cost, MWC, as used in Ballard *et al.* (1985) and Mayshar (1990), is defined as:

$$MWC = \frac{\Delta(EV) - \Delta R}{\Delta R} \tag{3.39}$$

Hence the marginal welfare cost is just the marginal cost of funds, minus 1, and:

$$MWC = MCF - 1 \qquad (3.40)$$

The extended Samuelson condition requires that the sum of marginal rates of substitution should exceed the product of the marginal rate of transformation and the marginal cost of funds. As Fullerton (1991, p.306) mentioned, the marginal welfare cost can be zero even for a distorting tax, if the distortion is compensated by a positive revenue effect. Furthermore, a lump sum tax may, starting from a distorted situation, increase or decrease the excess burden, depending on whether it reduces or increases the revenue from other taxes.

Following an extensive examination of alternative excess burden measures, Mayshar (1990, p.263) concluded that the marginal cost of funds, as defined above, 'should be regarded as the most useful concept in applied tax analysis'. However, this strong claim needs to be qualified: it is simply the relevant concept in balanced-budget studies, and is related in a very straightforward way to the marginal welfare cost (excess burden) that is relevant for differential incidence studies.

Related studies include Wildasin (1979) and Triest (1990). The relationship between the marginal cost of funds and tax evasion was examined by Usher (1986), and Fortin and Lacroix (1994) who compared the effects of tax increases with the use of higher penalties and a higher probability of detection. A detailed treatment of welfare costs and the cost of funds can also be found in Schob (1994), who introduced measures of the marginal benefit of public funds, along with modified measures of the marginal cost of funds, in an attempt to overcome the fact that standard measures of the marginal cost of funds require knowledge of the precise nature of the additional government expenditure. All these papers ignored distributional issues by using either identical individuals or a single individual.

The importance of the distinction between balanced budget and differential studies, along with the clarification of the role of the marginal cost of funds, are major points to arise from these analyses. The balanced budget

context only gives the same answer as the differential studies, corresponding to excess burden calculations, when the extra government expenditure
is equivalent to a cash transfer. A major lesson from the study of alternative models, culminating in the comparisons of Snow and Warren (1996)
mentioned above, is that the form of the model can have important implications for the numerical orders of magnitude of the measures. Of particular
importance is the issue of whether government expenditure affects labour
supply.

The particular formulae used to examine marginal welfare costs for very
small changes are perhaps of more practical value for the analysis of marginal
tax reforms. The expressions involve elasticities and single marginal tax
rates, and they do not require the form of the utility function to be specified. However, they are typically applied at the level of the representative
consumer, with users taking point estimates of elasticities from other studies.
In genuine applications, in contrast with theoretical comparisons, attention
needs to be given to population heterogeneity. The focus on a representative
consumer also means that distributional issues are entirely ignored, though
such issues may be an important consideration in realistic policy considerations. Even when using small general equilibrium models, the assumption
is usually made that there is a single individual supplying labour and de-
manding goods. These analyses may nevertheless be useful in enabling the
analysis to focus on some special cases.

The approximations can, as mentioned above, be applied at lower levels
of aggregation, given sufficient data for the estimation of demand systems.
Appeal can then perhaps be made to the lack of sensitivity of the first derivatives of estimated demand equations (at observed consumption levels) to the
functional form or restrictions imposed for estimation purposes, as an argument in favour of using approximations. But it seems to be the case that
those using the approximations are not prepared, for whatever reason, to
carry out the estimation themselves. Furthermore, given a set of estimates,
it is then only a small step to obtaining exact measures, as shown in the next
chapter. It is also worth making the point that few, if any, tax policies are
marginal; the most important are certainly not marginal.

3.6   Conclusions

This chapter has examined alternative concepts of the welfare cost of taxation. The major concepts of welfare change, including excess burdens and the marginal cost of funds, were discussed, with particular attention being paid to the case of income taxation where labour supplies are variable. Various approximations to the welfare measures were examined, including the analysis of marginal tax reforms. If it is desired to calculate exact measures rather than approximations, the major requirement in practical studies is an appropriate method of obtaining either the form of the expenditure functions or their numerical values in relevant situations. The required welfare changes for a fully specified change in the tax structure can then be calculated, for each population group for which estimates are available, and the major constraint on the number of groups is imposed by data limitations. Alternative approaches are discussed in the following chapter.

Chapter 4

Measuring Welfare Changes

The emphasis of this chapter is on empirical measurement issues. Attention is given to methods of producing exact welfare measures. The term 'exact' is used to distinguish measures from approximations, but it is not meant to indicate any special precision. The sampling properties of such measures need to be examined. Furthermore, in practice there is a need to allow for population heterogeneity, since individuals are in different circumstances and face different tax rates.

There are two broad approaches to providing an exact measure of welfare change for different population groups. One, discussed in section 4.1, is to use observed data in order to estimate the required parameters of a specified expenditure function by deriving the associated demand functions; the analytical or formal links between the expenditure functions and the demand functions are explicitly used. The expenditure function may be obtained by first specifying the form of the direct utility function; an example using the linear expenditure system is given. Alternatively the procedure may begin by specifying a form for the indirect utility function; an example using the 'almost ideal' demand system is given.

The second approach involves starting from an estimated form of Marshallian demand curve and moving from this to the required Hicksian demand curve, either by an algebraic method of integration or by a numerical method of integration. These approaches are discussed in section 4.2. Both the algebraic and numerical integration methods discussed in this section use

parametric estimates of consumer demand functions. The *a priori* imposition
of some structure makes it easier to estimate demand functions, particularly
using a limited amount of data. However, numerical methods of integration
can be applied to non-parametric estimates of demand functions, raising no
new basic welfare measurement issues; they are therefore not discussed here.

Given a set of estimates of expenditure functions for different population
groups, it may be desired to produce some kind of overall evaluation of a tax
policy change. This can be achieved using a specified social evaluation function, or welfare function, which is calculated using the distribution of equivalent incomes, following the approach explored by King (1983). The social
welfare function makes explicit the decision-maker's willingness to trade equity for efficiency. The use of equivalent incomes in this context is discussed
in section 4.3.

4.1   Direct and Indirect Utility Functions

This section discusses approaches to the estimation of the required expenditure functions. The first approach involves starting from the direct utility
function and deriving and then estimating the demand functions. The Marshallian demand functions can be derived by writing the form of the direct
utility function $U(x)$ and maximising subject to the constraint $m = \sum_i p_i x_i$.
The demand functions, and hence parameters of utility functions, are then
estimated using appropriate econometric methods. The substitution of the
demands $x^M(p, m)$ into $U(x)$ gives the indirect utility function $V(p, m)$. It is
then only necessary to invert the indirect utility function in order to obtain
the required expenditure function, $E(p, U)$; see chapter 2. The appropriate
terms required for the excess burdens can then be calculated directly.

The use of a direct utility function imposes a strong degree of structure,
which is particularly useful for estimation purposes when few data are available. An early study along these lines was made by Rosen (1978), who compared results using several specifications and estimation procedures. He used
the linear expenditure system, LES, estimated for a representative consumer
using time-series data, and the constant elasticity of substitution and LES

cases using household data. Rosen compared his aggregative measures with approximate measures, using approximations described above, but recognised that it is most unlikely that such approximations would actually be based on compensated elasticities calculated from a fully specified and estimated demand system. Subsection 4.1.1 shows how the approach via direct utility functions can be used in the context of the frequently used linear expenditure system.

One limitation of this direct utility approach is that solving the first-order conditions for utility maximisation is not straightforward except in a few well-known cases. The second approach involves starting from a specification of the indirect utility function (or, what amounts to the same thing, the expenditure function itself) and deriving and estimating the demand functions. The demand functions can then be estimated, thereby giving the required parameters of the expenditure functions. Subsection 4.1.2 illustrates this approach using the 'almost ideal' demand model.

4.1.1 The Linear Expenditure System

The linear expenditure system (LES) has additive utility functions of the form:

$$U = \prod_{i=1}^{n} (x_i - \gamma_i)^{\beta_i} \tag{4.1}$$

where γ_i is referred to as 'committed consumption', with $x_i > \gamma_i$, $0 \leq \beta_i \leq 1$, and $\sum_i \beta_i = 1$. Demand functions are given by:

$$p_i x_i = \gamma_i p_i + \beta_i \left(m - \sum_j p_j \gamma_j \right) \tag{4.2}$$

Substitution into U gives:

$$V(p, U) = (m - A) / B \tag{4.3}$$

where A and B are given by:

$$A = \sum_i p_i \gamma_i \tag{4.4}$$

$$B = \prod_i \left(\frac{p_i}{\beta_i}\right)^{\beta_i} \tag{4.5}$$

The expenditure function, $E(p, U)$, is given by rearranging equation (4.3) to give:

$$E(p, U) = A + BU \tag{4.6}$$

Hence the compensating variation is:

$$CV = A^1 + B^1 U^0 - m^0 \tag{4.7}$$

After substituting for U^0, this can be rearranged to give:

$$CV = A^0 \left[\frac{A^1}{A^0} + \frac{B^1}{B^0}\left(\frac{m^0}{A^0} - 1\right)\right] - y^0 \tag{4.8}$$

The term A^1/A^0 is equal to $\sum_i p_i^1 \gamma_i / \sum_i p_i^0 \gamma_i$ and is therefore a Laspeyres type of price index, using the committed consumption of each good as the weight. This form can be converted to allow for taxes, or proportional changes in prices. If $\dot{p}_i$ denotes the proportionate change in the price of the ith good, then $A^1/A^0 = 1 + \sum_i s_i \dot{p}_i$ where $s_i = p_i^0 \gamma_i / \sum_i p_i^0 \gamma_i$. In the case where a new *ad valorem* tax is introduced, then the proportional price change, $\dot{p}_i$, is equal to t_i. If a tax rate is increased by the absolute amount, Δt_i, then $\dot{p}_i = \Delta t_i / (1 + t_i)$.

The term B^1/B^0 in (4.8) simplifies to:

$$\frac{B^1}{B^0} = \prod_i \left(\frac{p_i^1}{p_i^0}\right)^{\beta_i} \tag{4.9}$$

which is a weighted geometric mean of price relatives. The equivalent variation is:

$$EV = m^1 - A^0 \left[1 + \frac{B^0}{B^1}\left(\frac{m^1}{A^0} - \frac{A^1}{A^0}\right)\right] \tag{4.10}$$

Given parameter estimates, the welfare changes can be calculated for each individual in a household expenditure survey, or for selected types of individual at specified income levels.

The linear expenditure system has been extensively used in empirical studies; see Powell (1974), Lluch *et al.* (1977), and Dixon *et al.* (1982) where it forms the basis of the demand side of a multi-sector general equilibrium model of Australia. Muellbauer (1974) used the LES to examine the welfare effects of inflation in the UK, where parameters were estimated for a representative household, although distributional implications are implied by the changes in the two types of price index. Stoker (1986) used the translog model to examine the welfare effects of inflation. In demand systems using a representative household, the total expenditure elasticities converge towards unity as total expenditure increases.

Dodgson (1983) used the LES, along with its special case of the Cobb-Douglas utility function, with parameters simply taken from average budget shares. The Cobb-Douglas is obtained from the LES by setting the committed expenditures to zero, so that the above results can easily be modified; both Muellbauer and Dodgson used Deaton's (1975) estimates of the LES. He compared the values of welfare change and excess burden, including the Harberger approximation, arising from indirect taxes in the UK. He found that for 14 commodity groups there was broad agreement between the measures of welfare change, but the Harberger approximation substantially overestimated the excess burden.

The assumption of additivity of the LES is very strong and implies, for example, that complementarity is ruled out and that own-price elasticities are approximately proportional to income elasticities; see Deaton (1974, 1975). The problems are generally thought to be less severe when broad commodity groups are used, though they often represent the cost of overcoming data limitations. The main data limitations usually relate to information about price responses at the required level of disaggregation. If all individuals are assumed to have the same parameters, one implication of the LES is that it gives rise to uniform optimal indirect taxes. However, it is possible to allow for heterogeneity. Instead of using a single set of parameters, welfare measures can be based on separate estimates of the LES for each of a range of total expenditure groups. Households within each group are assumed to have the same preferences, but these are allowed to vary with total expenditure. The uniformity of optimal indirect taxes does not arise with taste heterogeneity.

It is possible to obtain estimates of the parameters of the linear expenditure system for each of a variety of total expenditure groups, using only cross-sectional budget data; this is considered in detail in chapter 5. As suggested above, the strong *a priori* restrictions underlying this type of parametric approach represent the cost of obtaining a large number of demand elasticities with limited data. However, such a data limitation is a situation that faces many researchers who nevertheless need some idea of orders of magnitude in order to examine policy issues.

4.1.2   The Almost Ideal Demand System

This subsection discusses the 'almost ideal' demand system, proposed by Deaton and Muellbauer (1980). The derivation of this model begins by specifying the form of the indirect, rather than the direct, utility function.

First, it is useful to consider the logarithmic form of Shephard's lemma, which relates budget shares to the expenditure function. From Shephard's lemma the compensated demand for the ith good, x^H, can be obtained using $x^H = \partial E(p,U)/\partial p_i$. Hence, it can be seen that the budget share, $w_i = x_i p_i / y$, with $y = \sum_i p_i x_i = E(p,U)$, is given by:

$$w_i = \frac{\partial \log E(p,U)}{\partial \log p_i} \tag{4.11}$$

If the expenditure function takes the form:

$$\log E(p,U) = a(p) + b(p)U \tag{4.12}$$

where a and b are general functions of the prices, that is, they are particular types of price index, the associated budget shares are:

$$w_i = p_i \frac{\partial a(p)}{\partial p_i} + U p_i \frac{\partial b(p)}{\partial p_i} \tag{4.13}$$

This uses the general result that where $\log m = a\left(e^{\log x}\right)$, differentiating gives $\partial \log m / \partial \log x = (\partial a / \partial x)\left(\partial e^{\log x}/\partial \log x\right) = e^{\log x}(\partial a/\partial x) = x(\partial a/\partial x)$.

Writing the indirect utility as $U = (\log m - a)/b$, using (4.12), equation (4.13) can be expressed as:

$$w_i = p_i \frac{\partial a(p)}{\partial p_i} + \frac{p_i \partial b(p)}{b(p) \partial p_i} \log \left(\frac{m}{\exp a(p)} \right) \tag{4.14}$$

The 'almost ideal' demand system is obtained by specifying $a(p)$ and $b(p)$ as taking the following forms:

$$a(p) = \alpha_0 + \sum_k \alpha_k \log p_k + \frac{1}{2} \sum_k \sum_\ell \gamma_{k\ell}^* \log p_k \log p_\ell \tag{4.15}$$

$$b(p) = \beta_0 \prod_k p_k^{\beta_k} \tag{4.16}$$

The partial derivatives are therefore:

$$\frac{\partial a(p)}{\partial p_i} = \frac{1}{p_i} \left\{ \alpha_i + \frac{1}{2} \sum_k (\gamma_{ik}^* + \gamma_{ki}^*) \log p_i \right\} \tag{4.17}$$

and:

$$\frac{\partial b(p)}{\partial p_i} = \frac{\beta_i}{p_i} b(p) \tag{4.18}$$

Defining the price index $P = \exp a(p)$, and writing $\gamma_{ij} = \frac{1}{2} \left(\gamma_{ij}^* + \gamma_{ji}^* \right)$, the budget shares are given by:

$$w_i = \alpha_i + \sum_k \gamma_{ik} \log p_k + \beta_i \log \left(\frac{m}{P} \right) \tag{4.19}$$

Additivity requires $\sum_i \alpha_i = 1$, $\sum_k \gamma_{kj} = 0$ for all j, and $\sum_k \beta_k = 0$. In addition, homogeneity gives $\sum_k \gamma_{jk} = 0$ and symmetry gives $\gamma_{ij} = \gamma_{ji}$.

The price index, $P = \exp a(p)$, makes the budget shares highly nonlinear in the parameters, but if this can be approximated by a simple price index, the unrestricted form of the model can be estimated using ordinary least squares applied to each good in turn, using time series data.

Suppose prices change from p_0 to p_1. The equivalent variation, EV, is by definition $E(p_1, U_1) - E(p_0, U_1)$. Using $E(p_1, U_1) = m_1$ and:

$$U_1 = \frac{1}{b(p_1)} \log\left(\frac{m_1}{P_1}\right) \tag{4.20}$$

then, from (4.12):

$$EV = m_1 - \exp\{a(p_0) + b(p_0)U_1\} \tag{4.21}$$

and:

$$EV = m_1 - P_0 \exp\left\{\frac{b(p_0)}{b(p_1)} \log\left(\frac{m_1}{P_1}\right)\right\} \tag{4.22}$$

From (4.22), the ratio of the equivalent variation to the post-change income is given by:

$$\frac{EV}{m_1} = 1 - \exp\left\{\frac{b(p_0)}{b(p_1)} \log\left(\frac{m_1}{P_1}\right) - \log\left(\frac{m_1}{P_0}\right)\right\} \tag{4.23}$$

The price index $b(p_0)/b(p_1)$ is a weighted geometric mean of price relatives. If the price changes involve proportional changes of $\dot{p}_i$, then this index can be conveniently written as:

$$\frac{b(p_0)}{b(p_1)} = \prod_i (1 + \dot{p}_i)^{-\beta_i} \tag{4.24}$$

It is instructive to compare the above expressions for the linear expenditure and the almost ideal demand systems.

4.2   From Marshallian to Hicksian Demands

The approaches described in the previous section involve obtaining the parameters of fully specified expenditure functions which are analytically linked to the demand functions that are estimated using available data. The imposition of a great deal of structure may often be useful, or indeed necessary, particularly where few data are available. But if there are a great deal of data, there may be circumstances in which such an approach is regarded as being too restrictive in allowing insufficient flexibility. Without the need to link demand and expenditure functions explicitly, a wider range of functional forms for the demand functions could be estimated; see, for example, McKenzie (1983, p.40). There is also the real danger that the welfare change measures obtained may depend too strongly on the form of the *a priori* restrictions imposed on the direct or indirect utility function. This section describes two alternative approaches which begin from the specification of the Marshallian demand functions and work backwards to get the information required, that is the values of the expenditure function for given prices and utility levels.

4.2.1 Algebraic Integration

An approach that begins with the demand function was proposed by Mohring (1971), followed by Hause (1975) and explored further by Hausman (1981). This uses estimates of the Marshallian demand functions without reference to the direct utility function. Consider a single price change. Along any indifference curve, the total differential of the indirect utility function must be zero, so that:

$$\frac{\partial V}{\partial p_i} dp_i + \frac{\partial V}{\partial m} dm = 0 \tag{4.25}$$

which can be rearranged to give:

$$\frac{dm}{dp_i} = -\frac{\partial V/\partial p_i}{\partial V/\partial m} \tag{4.26}$$

But it is known from Roy's identity that the right-hand side of (4.26) is the Marshallian demand, $x^M(p, m)$. Hence the integration of $dm/dp_i = x^M(p, m)$, along with an appropriate initial condition (for the constant of integration), gives the required minimum expenditure associated with any given utility level and set of prices.

Hause (1975) illustrated this approach using the cases of linear and log-linear Marshallian demands. Mohring (1971, p.352) gave an example involving demand functions of the form $x = \alpha m/p$ (which are of course known to be associated with Cobb-Douglas preferences). Hausman (1981) gave several numerical examples using the following linear case in the context of labour supply.

For a two-good model in which all quantities are deflated by the price of the second good, the Marshallian demand for good 1, is, omitting the subscript:

$$x = \gamma + \alpha p + \delta m \qquad (4.27)$$

The differential equation to be solved is given by:

$$\frac{dm(p)}{dp} = \gamma + \alpha p + \delta m \qquad (4.28)$$

Giving the solution, where c is the constant of integration:

$$m(p) = c \exp(\delta p) - \frac{1}{\delta}\left(\alpha p + \frac{\alpha}{\delta} + \gamma\right) \qquad (4.29)$$

Hausman selected the initial utility level, U, as the constant of integration, c. Substituting U for c and E for m therefore immediately gives the desired expenditure function as:

$$E(p, U) = U \exp(\delta p) - \frac{1}{\delta}\left(\alpha p + \frac{\alpha}{\delta} + \gamma\right) \qquad (4.30)$$

The term γ can be allowed to depend on various characteristics of households, so that welfare changes can be calculated for different types of household. Blomquist (1983) used this function to examine welfare changes in Sweden, and provided (pp.191-194) a detailed examination of the preferences implied by linear labour supply curves. Larson (1988) extended the basic approach to deal with supply curves and the case of the welfare changes facing producers in the face of price and production uncertainty. Larson (1992) later used the linear demand function results to illustrate how welfare changes resulting from quality changes of non-market goods could be evaluated.

Hause (1975, p.15) referred to the welfare change measures obtained by this type of approach as 'spuriously precise "exact" welfare change measures', but Hausman (1981) showed how the standard errors of the estimated parameters of the Marshallian demands can be used to attach sampling errors to the welfare changes. Criticisms of Hausman's illustrative welfare estimates were made by Browning (1985) and Haveman et al. (1987), but these did not concern the basic method of integrating from the Marshallian demands.

4.2.2 Numerical Integration

In all but the simplest of cases, the explicit algebraic integration of the Marshallian demand functions is too awkward. However, it is possible to use an efficient numerical method of obtaining the Hicksian or compensated demands from the Marshallian demand function. Several procedures were suggested by McKenzie (1983), but they are rather awkward to use and seem to have received little attention. This subsection concentrates on examining a method introduced by Vartia (1983), although Balk (1995) showed that the method was also contained in a recently discovered article by Malmquist (1993) that was originally written in the 1950s. There is no need to be restricted to specifications for which explicit solutions to the integration problem can be obtained, along the lines indicated in the previous subsection.

There have, however, been few applications of the technique, despite the fact that numerous references have been made to Vartia's method by critics of the continued use of approximations to welfare changes. A rare application of the method was by Porter-Hudak and Hayes (1987) who examined welfare effects of the price rise resulting from the 1973 oil embargo. Bockstael and McConnell (1993) showed in principle how the method can be used in the context of public goods. Wright and Williams (1988) examined the use of the method in the context of gains from market stabilisation, allowing for various degrees of risk aversion.

Hausman and Newey (1995) explored the use of non-parametric estimation procedures instead of parameterising the Marshallian demand curve, along with a numerical method of integration that differs from that of Vartia. Creel (1997) used Vartia's method in combination with Fourier functional forms for demand. Varian (1982) devised a non-parametric method using an approach based on revealed preferences. However, these methods, particularly the latter, require extensive data.

The Vartia method provides an extremely rapid numerical procedure that can easily be programmed and offers a great deal of potential, allowing welfare measures to be produced easily from demand functions that have been estimated without reference to an underlying (direct or indirect) utility function and which cannot be integrated analytically. For this reason, the following description states the algorithm using what it is hoped is more transparent notation than that of Vartia, and illustrates the use of the method for a hypothetical example.

Suppose that the Marshallian demand functions of n goods have been estimated. As before, the initial prices are denoted by p_i^0, giving rise to initial quantities demanded of x_i^0, for $i = 1, ..., n$. The superscript M, for Marshallian, has been omitted here for convenience. The level of total expenditure is m^0. A tax change leads to a new set of prices, p_i^1, for which the new demands can easily be calculated from the Marshallian demand function; but the problem is to calculate the appropriate values of the expenditure function, $E(p, U)$. This involves moving along the required indifference curve.

The first step involves setting a number of intervals, N, into which the price ranges are to be divided. A higher value of N increases the accuracy of the procedure. Then, for each good, i, obtain the following ($N + 1$ element) price vectors, for $j = 1, ..., N + 1$:

$$p_i(j) = p_i^0 + k(j)\left(p_i^1 - p_i^0\right) \tag{4.31}$$

where:

$$k(j) = \frac{j-1}{N} \tag{4.32}$$

The method involves repeating the following iterative procedure for values of j from $j = 2$ up to $j = N + 1$. For each value of j, it is required to find the 'stable' value of m, say $m(j)$, and 'stable' values of demands, say $x_i(j)$, for each good. Each stage, s, requires repeated calculation of quantities demanded, $x_i^{j(s)}$ for the jth price in the interval and the adjusted value of m, say $m^{j(s)}$, using, for each good, i:

$$x_i^{j(s)} = x_i\left(p_1(j), ..., p_n(j), m^{j(s-1)}\right) \tag{4.33}$$

with:

$$m^{j(s)} = m\left(j-1\right) + 0.5 \sum_{i=1}^{n} \left\{x_i^{j(s)} + x_i\left(j-1\right)\right\} \left\{p\left(j\right) - p\left(j-1\right)\right\} \quad (4.34)$$

using $x_i\left(1\right) = x_i^0$ and $m\left(1\right) = m^0$. Furthermore, $m^{j(1)} = m\left(j-1\right)$. Equations (4.33) and (4.34) are repeated for as many stages as are required in order to obtain:

$$\left|m^{j(s)} - m^{j(s-1)}\right| \leq \delta \quad (4.35)$$

with the value of δ set arbitrarily small; stability is usually achieved rapidly for each j. Equation (4.33) is evaluated using the estimated set of demand equations. Once this convergence has been reached, then the 'stable' value of $m^{j(s)}$ and the associated demands $x_i^{j(s)}$ are used for the next, that is the $j+1$th, set of values, $m\left(j+1\right)$ and $x_i\left(j+1\right)$. In practice, care should be taken to avoid setting δ too small, even with large N; a value of $\delta = 0.00001$ is usually appropriate. The accuracy of the method depends mainly on the number of intervals used for any particular context; experiments quickly reveal the order of magnitude to use for N.

When the values for $j = N+1$ have been calculated, the resulting 'stable' values of m and the x_is are the compensated values of total expenditure and demands. Hence the final xs correspond to those that are on the indifference surface passing through the initial consumption bundle, but with the new set of prices. Importantly, the final value of m obtained corresponds to the value of the expenditure function $E\left(p^1, U^0\right)$. The compensating variation is therefore given by the difference between this final stable value and the initial value of total expenditure, m^0. In order to calculate $E\left(p^0, U^1\right)$, from which the equivalent variation can be calculated, it is necessary to repeat the whole exercise by going backwards from the price vector p^1 to the vector p^0. The exact sampling properties of the resulting estimates have not been obtained, but their precision was examined by Porter-Hudak and Hayes (1986, 1987).

4.2.3   A Three-good Example

Each step of the above procedure converges rapidly, so it is possible to compute the welfare changes extremely quickly for large N. In order to demonstrate the use of the method, suppose that, for a particular type of individual, the following Marshallian demands have been obtained, using standard econometric methods. For each of three goods $(i = 1, 2)$ assume that:

$$x_i^M = \frac{\theta_i m}{p_i} \tag{4.36}$$

Here the prices represent the tax-inclusive prices. These demand functions are known to arise from a Cobb-Douglas utility function and are chosen purely for convenience. The value of Vartia's method is that it can be applied to any set of demands.

Suppose that $\theta_1 = 0.35$, $\theta_2 = 0.45$ and $\theta_3 = 0.2$, $m = 100$, while the initial prices are equal to 1, 1.2 and 1.5 respectively for goods 1 to 3. Suppose that *ad valorem* taxes are imposed leading to new prices of 1.1, 1.32 and 1.8; that is, $t_i = 0.1$ for all i. The application of the above method (for $\delta = 0.00001$ and $N = 100$) gives the results shown in Table 4.1. The row labelled p^0 shows the Marshallian demands for the pre-tax prices, along with the Hicksian demands corresponding to post-tax utility, U^1; the latter are obviously lower than the former because $U^1 < U^0$. The row labelled p^1 shows the Marshallian demands for the post-tax prices, along with the Hicksian demands corresponding to pre-tax utility U^0. The final two columns of the table give the values of minimum total expenditure for each price and utility combination.

Using the results shown in Table 4.1, the compensating and equivalent variations resulting from the tax change are equal to 11.931 and 10.659 respectively. Using the values in the table, it can be found that the tax revenue is equal to 10.606, while the revenue that would be obtained from the Hicksian demands, for prices p^1 and utility U^0, is equal to 11.871. Hence the excess burden based on the compensating variation, B_C, is 0.060, while that based on the equivalent variation, B_E, is 0.053.

Table 4.1: Hypothetical Example of Vartia's Method

	Marshallian demands			Hicksian demands				E (p, U)	
	x_1^M	x_2^M	x_3^M	x_1^H	x_2^H	x_3^H			
				U^1				U^0	U^1
p^0	35	37.5	13.33	31.269	33.503	11.912		100	89.341
				U^0					
p^1	31.818	34.091	11.11	35.614	38.158	12.437		111.931	100

4.2.4 Income Taxation

Consider instead an individual consuming two goods and leisure, where the demand functions take the same form as above, but respecified in terms of full income, and leisure is the third good with $\theta_3 = 0.2$. In using Vartia's approach, the value of m must be replaced by the sum of non-wage income and the product of the net wage and the endowment of time. In the present example, the endowment of time has been normalised to unity. Suppose that non-wage income is fixed at 20, while the prices of the two goods are fixed at 1 and 1.2 respectively, and the wage rate is initially 100. Hence full income is initially 120. The demands for goods 1 and 2 and for leisure are found to be 42, 45 and 0.24 respectively. The introduction of a proportional income tax, at the rate of 0.2, reduces the full income to 100, reduces the demands for the two goods to 35 and 37.5, and increases the demand for leisure to 0.25.

Using Vartia's method, the (Hicksian) consumption levels giving the initial utility, after the introduction of the tax, are 40.167, 43.036 and 0.287 respectively, corresponding to a full income of 114.762. The compensation required for the tax is therefore 14.762. The (Hicksian) demands corresponding to the post-tax utility level, at the initial prices, are found to be 36.597, 39.2115 and 0.209 respectively, corresponding to a full income of 104.564. Avoiding the introduction of the tax would involve returning to the full income of 120, so in the post-tax position the individual would be prepared to pay the difference between 120 and 104.564, that is 15.436, in order to avoid the tax.

In practice, sets of demand functions, including labour supply functions, would be estimated for a large range of household types. The numerical integration method could then be applied to each of a number of hypothetical households, or to each household in a budget survey. Nonlinear budget constraints, leading to jumps and other discontinuities in labour supply functions, can be accommodated using Vartia's method.

In some cases, the effects of specified income tax changes may be the primary focus of analysis and only a set of labour supply functions may be available. The above method can easily be carried out without the need for any information about the demand functions for commodity groups. This is because, as seen from equation (4.34), the demands for those goods for which there is no price change are irrelevant. Hence the above income tax example could be repeated without any consideration of the commodity demands, giving precisely the same values for the excess burdens. Care must be taken when using a given labour supply function, specified for example in terms of hours worked corresponding to a wage specified perhaps as an hourly rate, to ensure that full income is defined appropriately. This requires the maximum number of hours worked to be given. In the above example, the endowment of time has been normalised to one unit. Obviously, leisure and not labour supply must be fed into the numerical procedure.

4.3   The Use of Equivalent Incomes

The previous two sections have discussed alternative methods of calculating welfare changes for particular population groups (distinguished by income and other characteristics). It may, however, be required to provide an overall evaluation of a change in the tax structure. Such an evaluation can be carried out using a specified social welfare function that reflects a judge's value judgements. This section discusses the use of welfare functions expressed in terms of the distribution of individuals', or households', equivalent incomes.

The concept of equivalent income was defined in chapter 2, when considering money metric utility functions defined in terms of the indirect utility function. It has been explored in detail by King (1983). Examples using this concept, allowing for labour supply variations, include Apps and Savage

(1989) who used the 'almost ideal' demand system of Deaton and Muellbauer (1980), and Fortin *et al.* (1993) who used the linear expenditure system. An early brief discussion of equivalent incomes using the linear expenditure system was provided by Roberts (1980).

4.3.1 The Equivalent Income Function

Equivalent income is defined, following King (1983), as the value of income, m_e, which, at some reference set of prices, p_r, gives the same utility as the actual income level. In terms of the indirect utility function, m_e is therefore defined by the equation:

$$V(p_r, m_e) = V(p, m) \qquad (4.37)$$

Using the expenditure or cost function gives:

$$m_e = E(p_r, V(p, m)) \qquad (4.38)$$

This may be written as:

$$m_e = F(p_r, p, m) \qquad (4.39)$$

where the function F is referred to as the equivalent income function. An advantage of the equivalent income concept is that comparisons are made using a fixed set of reference prices.

King (1983, pp.208-210) gave the equivalent income function for the utility functions generating linear demands, loglinear demands, and the almost ideal demand system of Deaton and Muellbauer (1980). He also stated the functions for the direct utility functions associated with the linear expenditure system and the indirect translog system. Consider, for example, the linear expenditure system. The above results can be used to show that:

$$m_e = A_r + \frac{B_r(m - A)}{B} \qquad (4.40)$$

Expanding the terms in A and B gives:

$$m_e = \sum_i p_{ri}\gamma_i + \left\{\prod_i \left(\frac{p_{ri}}{p_i}\right)^{\beta_i}\right\}\left\{m - \sum_j p_j\gamma_j\right\} \qquad (4.41)$$

Consider the use of pre-change prices as reference prices, so that $p_{ri} = p_{0i}$ for all i. Substitution into equation (4.41) shows immediately that pre-change equivalent incomes are the actual incomes and the post-change equivalent income is the value of actual income after the change less the value of the equivalent variation; that is, $m_e^1 = m^1 - EV$.

Equivalent incomes are, as in the example of the linear expenditure system given here, nonlinear functions of the estimated parameters of the utility functions. Their sampling properties can therefore be examined using approximations such as that given by Goldberger (1964); the standard errors of welfare measures using this type of approach were discussed by King (1983, pp.210-212).

4.3.2   Social Evaluations

The effect on a specified social welfare or evaluation function of a change in prices and incomes can be measured in terms of a change in the distribution of equivalent incomes. Values of the social welfare function can be calculated for a population group using a complete distribution of values of m_e^0 and m_e^1 so that, according to the value judgements implicit in the welfare function, a change can be judged in terms of its overall effect.

An initial analysis might, for example, examine the generalised Lorenz curves for the distributions of m_e^0 and m_e^1 to see if standard 'dominance' results apply; for a statement of the various dominance conditions, see Lambert (1993a, b). These give comparisons of social welfare involving a minimum of assumptions about the precise form of welfare function. If these results do not provide a complete ordering of the distributions, then fully specified welfare functions can be evaluated.

Consider, for example, the use of a social welfare function defined in terms of equivalent incomes, such that welfare per person, W, is given by:

$$W = \frac{1}{N} \sum_{i=1}^{N} \frac{m_{e,i}^{1-\varepsilon}}{1 - \varepsilon} \qquad (4.42)$$

where ε is the degree of constant relative inequality aversion of the judge. This has the abbreviated form, expressed in terms of the arithmetic mean, $\bar{m}_e$, and Atkinson's inequality measure, I_A, of equivalent income, given by:

$$W = \bar{m}_e \left(1 - I_A\right) \qquad (4.43)$$

This conveniently reflects the trade-off between mean income and its equality, or between 'equity and efficiency', that the judge finds acceptable. Alternative forms of the welfare function may of course be used. For example, welfare rationales are available for the use of (4.43) with the Gini inequality measure or extended Gini substituted for the Atkinson measure; on abbreviated welfare functions, see Lambert (1993b). In practice it would be useful to examine the implications of adopting a range of value judgements.

4.4 Review of Strategies

It is appropriate to consider the major lessons arising from the review of concepts and methods provided in this and the previous chapter. However, dogmatism is best avoided as this is obviously an area where many issues are matters of judgement and preferences. First, and most obviously, it seems worth repeating the point that anyone who has gone to the trouble of estimating a Marshallian demand curve for a particular good has the information required for the evaluation of compensating or equivalent variations resulting from a price change. This is true even if the estimates are not based on any explicit restrictions introduced by specifying the form of direct or indirect utility functions. In some cases, algebraic integration can be carried out, but in the majority of cases (particularly when changes in several prices are considered), numerical methods of integration are needed. Having estimated the demands, this type of integration can be carried out for a small additional cost of time, given a computer program for performing the necessary iterations.

4.4.1 The Level of Aggregation

An important issue concerns the level of aggregation to be used. In the context of income taxation, numerous studies have attempted to measure the overall burden of taxation or the marginal welfare cost of a small change in taxation, or the associated marginal cost of funds. The methods used are usually, though not always, based on representative individual models, so that a single number is produced, based on a single compensated labour supply elasticity and tax rate. In addition, the tax system is summarised by a proportional tax. Such aggregate measures are invariably based on an approximation to the welfare measure, and the value used for the elasticity is typically taken from another study. Such studies can be carried out relatively quickly at low cost, but can perhaps be regarded as providing illustrations rather than reliable estimates; in some cases they might even be described in pejorative terms as 'back of the envelope' calculations. The results are attractive to those who wish to emphasise the welfare cost of taxation in popular debate by stating that, for example, 'for every \$1 of income tax revenue, there is an excess burden of x cents'.

Such studies have nevertheless helped to clarify some of the concepts involved and have provided an idea of the sensitivity of results to the assumptions used. A high level of aggregation on the consumption side is used in general equilibrium models. These, being based on assumed preferences, produce exact welfare change measures and have the advantage that they are able to allow for changes in input prices that result from the reallocation of resources consequent on the tax change. However, it has proved to be extremely difficult to build general equilibrium models displaying substantial heterogeneity on the household side. Hence, in practice a trade-off is involved between the level of aggregation and the desire to handle factor price changes.

Any practical policy analysis inevitably involves the more complex tax and transfer systems generally found in industrialised countries. Hence it is necessary to allow explicitly for the fact that there is a wide dispersion of welfare costs across the population. Individuals differ in the tax rates they face. Furthermore, such rates are endogenous, since they depend on labour supply decisions. It is suggested that, whenever possible, it would be best to avoid using a high level of aggregation; for strong criticisms of the use of a high level of aggregation and representative individual models, see Hammond (1990). It would be useful to attempt to examine welfare changes for a wide range of individuals or households. Policy analysis, faced with the distribution of changes, can then introduce explicitly the required value judgements in an evaluation of the overall effect of a tax change. This means a concentration on the demand side and, as suggested above, a neglect of general equilibrium considerations. It may be that progress here can be made by finding some way of linking the outputs of models developed for general equilibrium and household analyses.

4.4.2 The Use of Approximations

The use of approximations raises somewhat different considerations and is not necessarily linked to the level of aggregation used. Such approximations are attractive because they give results that can be expressed in terms of demand elasticities which are evaluated at observed expenditure levels. It is not appropriate to think that the use of approximations is necessarily quicker or cheaper than the calculation of exact measures, except of course where elasticities are taken from other studies. Determination of the elasticities requires an extensive exercise in applied demand analysis that involves estimating a set of demand functions which could in fact be used to obtain exact measures.

The use of approximations is more likely to be motivated by the judgement that the estimated demand functions may be unreliable for extrapolation purposes. This may be combined with the view that the first derivatives of demand functions are perhaps not so sensitive to the precise functional form used. Sensitivity analysis is still strongly recommended and it must always be remembered that only marginal tax changes can be examined.

The approximations relate to individuals whose positions are considered to be described by tangency solutions. They cannot handle those individuals who are at corner solutions or who, as a result of price changes, move towards or away from corner solutions. Furthermore, it has to be recognised that there is a practical need for the welfare evaluation of tax and other policy changes that cannot sensibly be regarded as marginal. Examples of non-marginal changes include a partial tax shift from direct to indirect taxation, a flattening of the income tax structure by eliminating higher marginal rates, and introducing or eliminating a tax on a particular good. It is this type of change which also gives rise to most public debate. This raises the need for an approach in which the exact welfare changes imposed on different types of household, and arising from a fully specified set of tax changes, can be evaluated. The model must be able to capture, as far as possible, the complexity of actual tax and transfer systems in operation. However, the special sense in which the term 'exact' is used in this context needs to be recognised; attention needs to be given to sampling variations.

4.4.3   The Importance of the Demand Model

As discussed in some detail in this chapter, the essential ingredient for the calculation of welfare measures is a method of evaluating expenditure functions. This can be achieved either by moving from the direct or indirect utility function to specification and estimation of the demand functions (and hence parameters of utility functions), or by integrating from estimated demand functions that have been obtained without imposing such strong *a priori* restrictions. The choice of approach will be substantially influenced by the nature of the available data.

Attempts to examine income tax changes present special problems because of the added complexity of the nonlinear budget constraints, although if the focus is on income taxation it is not necessary simultaneously to model the complexity of commodity demands. As stressed by King (1987, p.62), 'the quality of the model and associated parameter estimates is the critical factor in assessing the plausibility of the simulated gains and losses'. The model provides the foundation for welfare analysis. The question of the appropriate concepts to use in measuring welfare changes has been extensively debated and does not present the major practical challenge.

The real problems in and costs of any practical study arise from the difficulties of obtaining the demand model, including leisure demand. Ideally, the construction of a suitable model would begin (in the absence of longitudinal data) with a substantial data set consisting of a time series of household expenditure surveys, where information is available about labour supply as well as the various income sources, along with a time series of price indices for the same commodity groups as used in the cross-sectional budget surveys. The resulting large data set would enable a reasonable degree of disaggregation in estimating demand and labour supply functions. The production, cleaning and preparation of such a data set is an extensive and important exercise which should not be discounted. The luxury of being able to use this kind of resource is in fact available in only a few countries.

The specification and estimation of a demand and labour supply model then represents a major challenge, requiring careful judgement and a range of applied econometric skills. This usually requires a considerable degree of experimentation with alternative approaches; one approach is seldom unambiguously superior to others. In general, more structure has to be imposed if available data, particularly regarding price responses, are limited. For surveys of applied demand analysis see, for example, Deaton (1986), Blundell (1988), Blundell *et al.* (1993) and Clements *et al.* (1996).

Having produced and estimated a suitable demand model, the next step involves the production of computer software which is capable of applying particular tax structures to a sample of households and evaluating the welfare changes for each household. A variety of distributional analyses can then be carried out, including the study of detailed effects for particular types of household, the production of inequality measures and the examination of alternative social evaluation functions which embody explicit value judgements. This kind of project inevitably involves a certain amount of team work drawing on a range of skills, including computing skills. It is therefore not surprising that the best examples of this type of work have come from special research centres or groups relying on substantial grants.

4.5   Conclusions

This chapter examined alternative approaches to the practical measurement
of exact welfare changes. These included approaches based on the specification of either the direct or the indirect utility function, and the derivation
of associated demand functions that are then estimated. Alternatively, unrestricted estimates of Marshallian demand functions can be used, where the
required values of expenditure functions are obtained either by algebraic or
numerical integration methods. Finally, the evaluation of tax changes using a
social welfare function defined in terms of equivalent incomes was discussed.

   The fundamental requirement of any detailed practical analysis of welfare changes is a suitable consumer demand model, along with empirical
estimates of the required demand functions including, where relevant, labour
supply functions. Data constraints are therefore likely to play a crucial role
in determining the choice of approach.

Chapter 5

A Convenient Parametric Approach

This chapter describes a method of estimating the welfare effects of a set of price changes, using money measures of welfare change such as compensating and equivalent variations, and the associated concept of equivalent income. These concepts were discussed in chapters 3 and 4. The method is based on the explicit use of direct utility functions and is therefore 'parametric'. It involves the use of the linear expenditure system, LES, which is a special case of an additive demand system; this was discussed in chapter 4. At the cost of a little repetition, the present chapter is largely self contained. One serious limitation of the LES, when a single set of parameters is used, is that its implications for optimal indirect taxes are very strong, since it gives rise to uniform indirect taxes.

The approach presented here explicitly allows for heterogeneity. Instead of using a single set of parameters, the welfare measures are based on estimates of the LES for each of a range of total expenditure groups. Households within each group are assumed to have the same preferences, but these are allowed to vary with total expenditure. The uniformity of optimal indirect taxes does not arise with taste heterogeneity. It is shown how estimates of the parameters of the linear expenditure system can be obtained, for each of a variety of total expenditure groups, using only cross-sectional budget data. The strong *a priori* restrictions underlying this parametric approach represent the cost of obtaining a very large number of demand elasticities with limited data. However, such a data limitation is a situation that faces many researchers who nevertheless need some idea of orders of magnitude in order to examine policy issues.

The estimation of the linear expenditure system is described in section 5.1. The approach, involving a single set of expenditure weights for a variety of total expenditure groups, has no degrees of freedom because different parameters are obtained for each group; hence standard sampling statistics cannot be obtained. Section 5.2 shows how the set of estimated parameters can be used to calculate several welfare measures. The information needed to examine the welfare effects of differential price changes involves only proportionate price changes for each commodity group, so that price levels for each commodity group are not needed. Section 5.3 discusses the use of budget data. The application of the approach typically involves many elasticities; with n commodity groups and K total expenditure groups, there are Kn^2 own and cross-price elasticities. In order to illustrate the approach, a small numerical example is given.

5.1   The LES and Estimation

5.1.1   Demand Functions and Elasticities

The linear expenditure system (LES) has additive utility functions of the form:

$$U = \prod_{i=1}^{n} (x_i - \gamma_i)^{\beta_i} \qquad (5.1)$$

where x_i denotes the consumption of the ith good and γ_i is the committed consumption, with $x_i > \gamma_i, 0 \le \beta_i \le 1$. The normalisation $\sum_i \beta_i = 1$ is also imposed. The maximisation of utility subject to the budget constraint $m = \sum_i p_i x_i$ gives rise to the linear expenditure function for each good, i, of the form:

$$p_i x_i = \gamma_i p_i + \beta_i \left(m - \sum_j p_j \gamma_j \right) \qquad (5.2)$$

This can be rewritten in the more succinct form:

$$x_i^* = \frac{\beta_i m^*}{p_i} \qquad (5.3)$$

where $m^* = m - \sum_j p_j \gamma_j$ is called supernumerary income, and $x_i^* = x_i - \gamma_i$ is called the supernumerary consumption of good i; for an extensive treatment of the linear expenditure system see Powell (1974). The form of the expenditure functions given in equation (5.3) shows the relationship between results for the linear expenditure system and those obtained using the Cobb-Douglas form of utility function, where the latter is expressed in supernumerary terms. As discussed in chapters 2 and 4, allowance for variable labour supply can be made by including leisure as one of the goods, with a corresponding price equal to the net wage rate, and suitably redefining m as full income, that is, the maximum income obtained if no leisure were consumed; see Creedy (1994, 1996). However, the following analysis assumes that labour supplies are fixed, and m is referred to as total expenditure.

From differentiation of each expenditure function, given in equation (5.2), the own-price elasticity of demand for the ith good, η_{ii}, is given by:

$$\eta_{ii} = -\frac{\beta_i}{p_i x_i} \left(m - \sum_{j \neq i} p_j \gamma_j \right)$$

After some rearrangment this can be written more simply as:

$$\eta_{ii} = \frac{\gamma_i (1 - \beta_i)}{x_i} - 1 \qquad (5.4)$$

The cross-price elasticity, η_{ij}, that is the elasticity of demand for good i in response to a change in the price of good j, for all i, j pairs, is expressed as:

$$\eta_{ij} = \frac{\beta_i \gamma_j p_j}{p_i x_i}$$

This can usefully be written in the form:

$$\eta_{ij} = -\frac{\beta_i \gamma_j}{x_j} \left(\frac{w_j}{w_i} \right) \qquad (5.5)$$

where the term $w_i = p_i x_i / m$ is the expenditure or budget share of the ith good. The total expenditure elasticity of good i, e_i, is given by:

$$e_i = \frac{\beta_i m}{p_i x_i}$$

Using the definition of w_i, this becomes:

$$e_i = \frac{\beta_i}{w_i} \tag{5.6}$$

5.1.2   Estimation for Each Total Expenditure Group

As mentioned in the introduction, the linear expenditure system is not able
to describe the complex pattern of expenditure variations with total expenditure, particularly the observed non-monotonic convergence of expenditure
elasticities to unity, with a single set of β_i and γ_i, related, say, to a representative household with average income. The implications for indirect taxes of
assuming taste homogeneity are also very restrictive. However, the present
approach is to examine tax and distributional issues by making allowance for
variations in the βs and γs as total expenditure varies.

Suppose that household budget data are available giving, for each of a
range of total expenditure groups, the expenditure weights or budget shares,
w_i, for each commodity group. These weights can be used to find, for each
total expenditure group, the set of total expenditure elasticities, e_i, as explained below. Having calculated the e_is, the corresponding values of β_i can
be obtained using the relationship given in equation (5.6), so that:

$$\beta_i = e_i w_i \tag{5.7}$$

Consider the calculation of committed expenditure, $p_i \gamma_i$, for each commodity group and total expenditure or income group. If a value of the
own-price elasticity of demand is available using extraneous information for
each good at each income level, then equation (5.4) can be used, after rearrangement, since:

$$p_i \gamma_i = \frac{m w_i (1 + \eta_{ii})}{1 - \beta_i} \tag{5.8}$$

The required set of own-price elasticities, η_{ii}, may be obtained using a result established by Frisch (1959) for directly additive utility functions. The expressions require the use of the elasticity of the marginal utility of total expenditure with respect to total expenditure, ξ, often referred to as the 'Frisch parameter'. If δ_{ij} denotes the Kroneker delta, such that $\delta_{ij} = 0$ when $i \neq j$, and $\delta_{ij} = 1$ when $i = j$, then Frisch showed that the elasticities can be written as:

$$\eta_{ij} = -e_i w_j \left(1 + \frac{e_j}{\xi}\right) + \frac{e_i \delta_{ij}}{\xi} \tag{5.9}$$

so that the own-price elasticities are:

$$\eta_{ii} = e_i \left\{ \frac{1}{\xi} - w_i \left(1 + \frac{e_i}{\xi}\right) \right\} \tag{5.10}$$

These expressions are derived in the appendix to this chapter.

5.1.3 Frisch Parameters

The expression in (7.9) allows the price elasticities to be calculated using only household budget data for the w_is. But such data cannot provide direct estimates of the Frisch parameter. It is therefore necessary to make use of extraneous information.

For a review of earlier estimates of the Frisch parameter, see Brown and Deaton (1973). Tulpule and Powell (1978) used a value of $\xi = -1.82$ when calculating elasticities at average income for Australia, based on work of Williams (1978), and this value was adopted by Dixon et al. (1982) in calibrating a general equilibrium model. However, the relevant question in the present context is whether the Frisch parameter varies with income and, if so, the form of such variation. Frisch (1959, p.189) himself argued that the parameter would indeed vary with income, and he went so far as to state the following values as being applicable: -10 for the very poor; -2 for the 'median part' of the population; -0.7 for the 'better off 'part; and -0.1 for the 'richer' part. However, it is not clear how Frisch determined these values, and in the case of the LES, the minimum absolute value must be unity if the γs are positive.

Some empirical support for Frisch's conjecture was found by Lluch *et al.* (1977), based on variations across countries with different levels of GNP per capita. They concluded that their results 'conform with Frisch's 1959 conjecture that the expenditure elasticity of the marginal utility of income is negative, declines in absolute value with GNP per capita, and lies in the interval (-10, -0.1)' (1977, p.78). They also suggested, based on log-linear regression analysis, that it 'declines by approximately 0.36 per cent for every one per cent increase in GNP per capita' (1977, p.76). The same authors also examined within-country variations across urban and farm households and concluded that the 'conjecture of a negative relation between [ξ] and income is supported. In fact the estimated relation is not only negaive but relatively stable' (1977, p.250). Rimmer (1995) used a linear variation in the reciprocal of ξ with income.

On the basis of these findings, one approach involves using a flexible specification which extends the logarithmic form used by Lluch *et al.* (1977), whereby the variation in ξ with m is given by:

$$\log\left(-\xi\right) = a - \alpha \log\left(m + \theta\right) \qquad (5.11)$$

In practice, an indication of appropriate orders of magnitude for the parameters in (5.11) can be obtained by taking a set of assumed combinations of ξ and m, informed by the earlier results quoted above, and estimating (5.11) using a nonlinear method. The resulting parameters can form the basis of a range of sensitivity analyses. It may be necessary to impose a minimum absolute value of ξ that is somewhat higher than 1, in order to ensure that all the committed expenditures are positive.

With a choice of coefficients to use in equation (5.11), along with a set of budget shares for a variety of total expenditure groups, the results in the previous subsection can be used to calculate the values of β_i and $p_i\gamma_i$ for each of a range of total expenditure groups. These results, along with proportionate price changes, are sufficient to calculate the welfare effects of any specified change in the tax structure, as shown in the following section. First, the following subsection shows how the elasticities can be used to obtain new levels of expenditure resulting from a set of price changes. This is useful when the price changes are considered to arise from indirect tax changes, since total tax revenue needs to be considered, especially if revenue-neutral changes are appropriate. 'Non-welfarist' distributional measures may also be based on the distribution of net expenditure, that is gross expenditure less the indirect tax paid.

5.1.4 New Expenditure Levels

Holding m constant and differentiating the demand function for good i with respect to the prices gives:

$$\dot{x}_i = \sum_{j=1}^{n} \eta_{ij}\dot{p}_j \tag{5.12}$$

where the dots indicate proportionate changes. The new level of expenditure on the ith good may be denoted m_i. Hence, following the price changes, it is given by $m_i = p_i x_i + d(p_i x_i)$ where the total differential $d(p_i x_i)$ is equal to $p_i dx_i + x_i dp_i = p_i x_i (\dot{x}_i + \dot{p}_i)$. Substituting for $\dot{x}_i$ using equation (5.12), and noting that the initial expenditure on the good is equal to mw_i, gives:

$$m_i = mw_i \left(1 + \dot{p}_i + \sum_j \eta_{ij}\dot{p}_j\right) \tag{5.13}$$

Further insight into the relationship between m_i and the elasticity of demand for good i can be obtained by decomposing the cross-price elasticities, η_{ij}, using standard results from demand analysis. In particular, as shown in chapter 2, the income-compensated elasticities, σ_{ij}, are obtained from the Slutsky equation $\sigma_{ij} = \eta_{ij} + e_i w_j$. Furthermore, the substitution elasticities, s_{ij}, are given by $s_{ij} = \sigma_{ij}/w_j$.

Hence the price elasticities, η_{ij}, can be written as:

$$\eta_{ij} = (s_{ij} - e_i) w_j \tag{5.14}$$

Substituting for η_{ij} from equation (5.14) into the expression for m_i in equation (5.13) gives:

$$m_i = mw_i \left(1 + \dot{p}_i + \sum_j \dot{p}_j \, w_j s_{ij} - e_i \sum_j \dot{p}_j \, w_j \right) \qquad (5.15)$$

This shows how the new expenditure on good i depends on the substitution arising from the changes in relative prices and an income effect. If all prices change by the same proportion then $\dot{p}_j = \dot{p}$ for all j. The adding-up condition $\sum_i w_i e_i = 1$ can be used along with the homogeneity condition $\sum_j w_j s_{ij} = 0$ to give:

$$m_i = mw_i \left\{ 1 + \dot{p}(1 - e_i) \right\} \qquad (5.16)$$

Hence in this case m_i depends only on the income elasticity of demand for good i.

5.2   Welfare Effects

Given estimates of β_i and $p_i\gamma_i$ for each commodity and total expenditure group, it is required to obtain welfare effects for specified proportionate price changes, assuming all consumers face the same prices. This section shows how compensating and equivalent variations, and equivalent incomes, can be calculated. These terms require the use of an expression giving the minimum cost of achieving a specified level of utility at a given set of prices. This relationship is given by the expenditure function. This has been derived for the LES in chapter 4 but is repeated in the following subsection for completeness.

5.2.1   The Expenditure Function

The first stage in obtaining the expenditure function is to derive the indirect utility function, $V(p, m)$, which expresses utility as a function of prices and income and is obtained by substituting the solution for the demands, given in equation (5.3), into the utility function of equation (5.1). Hence, as shown in chapter 4:

$$V(p, U) = (m - A)/B \tag{5.17}$$

where the terms A and B are given by:

$$A = \sum_i p_i \gamma_i \tag{5.18}$$

$$B = \prod_i \left(\frac{p_i}{\beta_i}\right)^{\beta_i} \tag{5.19}$$

This is the form of the indirect utility function for the linear expenditure system given by Allen (1975), in the context of examining the differential impact of inflation on different income groups, as in Muellbauer (1974). However, he did not allow the parameters γ and β to vary with total expenditure.

The expenditure function is the minimum expenditure required to achieve utility U at prices p, written as $E(p, U)$. It is given by rearranging equation (5.17), that is inverting the indirect utility function, to give:

$$E(p, U) = A + BU \tag{5.20}$$

5.2.2 Compensating and Equivalent Variations

Suppose that prices change from p_0 to p_1 as a result of the imposition of indirect taxes. The compensating variation, CV, is the difference between the minimum expenditure required to achieve the original utility level, at the new prices, and the initial total expenditure. Hence in the context of a price rise it is the amount that needs to be given to an individual in order to restore the original utility level, at the new prices. Hence:

$$CV = E(p_1, U_0) - E(p_0, U_0) \tag{5.21}$$

Using equation (5.20) and adding subscripts to indicate the relevant set of prices, this becomes:

$$CV = A_1 + B_1 U_0 - m_0 \tag{5.22}$$

After substituting for $U_0 = (m_0 - A_0)/B_0$, this can be rearranged to give:

$$CV = A_0 \left[\frac{A_1}{A_0} + \frac{B_1}{B_0} \left(\frac{m_0}{A_0} - 1 \right) \right] - m_0 \qquad (5.23)$$

The term A_1/A_0 is equal to $\sum_i p_{1i}\gamma_i / \sum_i p_{0i}\gamma_i$ and is therefore a Laspeyres type of price index, using the committed consumption of each good as the weight. For this reason it is sometimes referred to as a price index of 'necessities'.

Since actual prices are not usually available, it is necessary to convert this form of the price index into one involving only proportional changes in prices. If $\dot{p}_i$ denotes the proportionate change in the price of the ith good, then $p_{1i} = p_{0i}(1 + \dot{p}_i)$ and:

$$\frac{A_1}{A_0} = 1 + \sum_i s_i \dot{p}_i \qquad (5.24)$$

where the term s_i is defined as:

$$s_i = \frac{p_{0i}\gamma_i}{\sum_i p_{0i}\gamma_i} \qquad (5.25)$$

The term B_1/B_0 in (5.23) simplifies to:

$$\frac{B_1}{B_0} = \prod_i \left(\frac{p_{1i}}{p_{0i}} \right)^{\beta_i} \qquad (5.26)$$

which is interpreted as a weighted geometric mean of price relatives. It is sometimes referred to as reflecting the price of 'luxuries'. Again it is necessary to express this in terms of the proportionate changes, so that:

$$\frac{B_1}{B_0} = \prod_i (1 + \dot{p}_i)^{\beta_i} \qquad (5.27)$$

Equation (5.23) is used, with equations (5.24) and (5.27), to calculate the compensating variation, given a set of proportionate price changes and the coefficients β_i, along with the initial cost of committed expenditure for each good, $p_i\gamma_i$. An important feature of the results is that the precise values of γ_i and p_i are not required.

The equivalent variation is the difference between the post-change total expenditure and the minimum expenditure required to achieve post-change

utility at the pre-change prices. It is the compensating variation corresponding to a price change in the opposite direction. Hence:

$$EV = E(p_1, U_1) - E(p_0, U_1) \qquad (5.28)$$

This can be written as:

$$EV = m_1 - (A_0 + B_0 U_1) \qquad (5.29)$$

Substituting for $U_1 = (m_1 - A_1)/B_1$ into equation (5.29) and rearranging
gives:

$$EV = m_1 - A_0 \left[1 + \frac{B_0}{B_1} \left(\frac{m_1}{A_0} - \frac{A_1}{A_0} \right) \right] \qquad (5.30)$$

This expression may be compared with the compensating variation given
in equation (5.23). The two price indices A_1/A_0 and B_1/B_0 may again be
obtained using equations (5.24) to (5.27).

5.2.3 Equivalent Incomes

An alternative approach to the measurement of the distributional effects of
price changes, also discussed in chapter 4, involves the use of the distribution
of equivalent incomes. Equivalent income is defined as the value of income,
m_e, which, at some reference set of prices, p_r, gives the same utility as the
actual income level. In terms of the indirect utility function, m_e is therefore
defined by the equation:

$$V(p_r, m_e) = V(p, m) \qquad (5.31)$$

Using the expenditure or cost function gives:

$$m_e = E(p_r, V(p, m)) \qquad (5.32)$$

This may be written as:

$$m_e = F(p_r, p, m) \qquad (5.33)$$

where the function F is referred to as the equivalent income function. For the linear expenditure system, this can be obtained using equations (5.20) and (5.17). The actual utility, U, can be expressed from the indirect utility function as $(m - A)/B$. The minimum expenditure required to achieve this utility level, at the reference set of prices, is given by:

$$m_e = A_r + \frac{B_r\,(m - A)}{B} \tag{5.34}$$

Expanding the terms in A and B gives:

$$m_e = \sum_i p_{ri}\gamma_i + \left\{ \prod_i \left(\frac{p_{ri}}{p_i} \right)^{\beta_i} \right\} \left\{ m - \sum_j p_j\gamma_j \right\} \tag{5.35}$$

The effect on welfare of a change in prices and income can then be measured in terms of a change in equivalent incomes, from m_{0e} to m_{1e}, where, as before, the indices 0 and 1 refer to pre-change and post-change values respectively. From this, changes in welfare at different income levels can be compared. Furthermore, values of a social welfare function can be obtained for a population group using values of m_{0e} and m_{1e} so that, according to the value judgements implicit in the welfare function, a change can be judged in terms of its overall effect.

An important feature of the equivalent income function is that it ensures that alternative tax policies are evaluated using a common set of reference prices. Consider the use of pre-change prices as reference prices, so that $p_{ri} = p_{0i}$ for all i. Substitution into equation (5.35) shows immediately that pre-change equivalent incomes are simply the actual incomes, and thus $m_{0e} = m_0$. Equivalent incomes after the change in the tax structure are given by:

$$m_{1e} = \sum_i p_{0i}\gamma_i + \left\{ \prod_i \left(\frac{p_{0i}}{p_{1i}} \right)^{\beta_i} \right\} \left\{ m_1 - \sum_j p_{1j}\gamma_j \right\} \tag{5.36}$$

This can be written as:

$$m_{1e} = A_0 \left[1 + \frac{B_0}{B_1} \left(\frac{m_1}{A_0} - \frac{A_1}{A_0} \right) \right] \tag{5.37}$$

Comparison of equations (5.30) and (5.37) shows that when the reference prices are equal to the pre-change prices, the post-change equivalent income is the value of actual income after the change less the value of the equivalent variation; that is, $m_{1e} = m_1 - EV$.

5.3   The Use of Budget Data

The first stage in calculating the price elasticities for each total expenditure level requires information about the way in which the w_is and e_is vary with income. Most standard demand systems, applied to 'representative households', imply that the income elasticities, e_i, converge steadily to unity as income increases. However, the present approach does not estimate a precise relationship, but uses the values obtained directly from the household budget data.

The income or total expenditure elasticities can be expressed in terms of changes in expenditure weights. Using the basic definition $w_i = p_i q_i / m$, differentiation gives:

$$\dot{w}_i = \dot{m}\left(e_i - 1\right) \tag{5.38}$$

where $\dot{w}_i$ denotes the proportional change in the expenditure weight on the ith good, dw_i / w_i, resulting from the proportional change in total expenditure, $dm/m = \dot{y}$. Rearranging this result gives:

$$e_i = 1 + \dot{w}_i / \dot{m} \tag{5.39}$$

From budget data it is possible to calculate, for each commodity group, the average expenditure weights for, say, K total expenditure groups. These weights can be arranged in the form of a matrix with K rows and n columns. Denote the midpoints of the K total expenditure groups by m_k $(k = 1, ..., K)$ and the expenditure weight for the ith commodity group and kth total expenditure group by w_{ki} $(i = 1, ..., n)$.

Define the following proportionate changes, for $k = 2, ..., K$:

$$\dot{m}'_k = (m_{k-1}/m_k) - 1 \tag{5.40}$$

$$\dot{w}'_{ki} = (w_{k-1,i}/w_{ki}) - 1 \qquad (5.41)$$

Although the 'dot' notation has been used, the above proportionate changes are discrete changes, obtained by comparing values in adjacent total expenditure groups. These can be used to substitute into equation (5.39) to get the set of total expenditure elasticities for $k = 2, ..., K$ and $i = 1, ..., n$, giving:

$$e'_{i(k)} = 1 + \dot{w}'_{ki}/\dot{m}'_k \qquad (5.42)$$

Similarly, for $k = 1, ..., K - 1$ define the proportionate changes:

$$\dot{m}^*_k = (m_{k+1}/m_k) - 1 \qquad (5.43)$$

$$\dot{w}^*_{ki} = (w_{k+1,i}/w_{ki}) - 1 \qquad (5.44)$$

$$e^*_{i(k)} = 1 + \dot{w}^*_{ki}/\dot{m}^*_k \qquad (5.45)$$

The arithmetic mean values of (5.42) and (5.45) can be used for $k = 2, ..., K - 1$, while (5.42) and (5.45) can be used respectively for $k = K$ and $k = 1$. In practice, the raw budget shares for each commodity group are likely to display too much variability, giving rise to some negative total expenditure elasticities. This can be overcome by smoothing the data, though this must be done very carefully since additivity must be ensured.

5.3.1   Numerical Examples

In practice the application of the above procedures involves a very large number of elasticities. Furthermore, the examination of welfare changes using equivalent incomes may involve the use of total expenditure levels for a large number of individual households (either from a household expenditure survey or from a simulated distribution). Practical examples are given in part III of this book, but in order to illustrate the approach, the present section uses a hypothetical set of data.

Table 5.1: Expenditure Weights

m	w_1	w_2	w_3	w_4
50	0.480	0.190	0.200	0.130
60	0.450	0.185	0.215	0.150
70	0.400	0.165	0.235	0.200
80	0.385	0.155	0.245	0.215
90	0.380	0.150	0.250	0.220

It is necessary, given household budget data, to calculate expenditure weights for each of a range of total expenditure groups and for each commodity group. These can be placed in a matrix, as in Table 5.1, which shows a hypothetical set of weights for four commodities and five total expenditure groups. The midpoints of the total expenditure groups are assumed to have values of [50, 60, 70, 80, 90], and the upper limits of each class are assumed to be [55, 65, 75, 85, 95]. The weights of the first two commodities decline as total expenditure increases, whereas those for the last two commodities increase with total expenditure. The row sums are of course unity.

The weights in Table 5.1 are then used to obtain the total expenditure and own-price elasticities shown in Table 5.2. The total expenditure elasticities do not converge monotonically towards zero as total expenditure increases. In order to compute the own-price elasticities in Table 5.2, it is necessary to make an assumption about the variation in ξ. The values are based on the assumption that they follow the logarithmic profile:

$$\log\left(-\xi\right) = 5 - 0.5 \log m \qquad (5.46)$$

In practice it is necessary to ensure that the implied values of committed expenditure are positive; this may involve imposing a minimum absolute value of ξ for the highest total expenditure group. The income elasticities are then used to obtain the values of β_i for each income group, using equation (5.7). These values are shown in Table 5.3. The values of β_i show directly the proportion of supernumerary income devoted to the supernumerary expenditure of each good. Table 5.3 also shows the values of committed expenditure for each commodity and total expenditure group. These committed expen-

Table 5.2: Total Expenditure and Own-price Elasticities

m	e_1	e_2	e_3	e_4	η_{11}	η_{22}	η_{33}	η_{44}
50	0.687	0.868	1.375	1.769	-0.352	-0.200	-0.322	-0.295
60	0.467	0.595	1.488	2.400	-0.229	-0.138	-0.373	-0.440
70	0.431	0.364	1.447	2.137	-0.193	-0.079	-0.394	-0.496
80	0.792	0.613	1.245	1.372	-0.338	-0.128	-0.357	-0.353
90	0.882	0.700	1.180	1.205	-0.372	-0.145	-0.348	-0.322

Table 5.3: Betas and Committed Expenditures

m	β_1	β_2	β_3	β_4	$\gamma_1 p_1$	$\gamma_2 p_2$	$\gamma_3 p_3$	$\gamma_4 p_4$
50	0.330	0.165	0.275	0.230	23.21	9.11	9.34	5.95
60	0.210	0.110	0.320	0.360	26.34	10.76	11.90	7.87
70	0.173	0.060	0.340	0.428	27.32	11.31	15.11	12.31
80	0.305	0.095	0.305	0.295	29.33	11.94	18.13	15.78
90	0.335	0.105	0.295	0.265	32.27	12.90	20.80	18.28

ditures are seen to rise with total expenditure, as expected.

Consider the welfare effects of imposing a set of indirect tax rates on the goods. Suppose that a tax-exclusive rate of 0.15 is imposed on goods three and four, while goods one and two are exempt from tax. Starting from a situation in which there are no taxes, this implies that the proportionate change in the price of goods three and four is in each case equal to 0.15, on the assumption that the tax is fully passed on to consumers. This assumes also that only direct effects of the tax changes are relevant. In a more complex situation it may be necessary to consider any indirect effects, if any taxed good is used as an input in the production of other goods. Such indirect effects on prices can be calculated using information about the extent of inter-industry transactions shown by the input-output matrix. In view of the variation in the budget shares shown in Table 5.1, it is expected that this tax structure will impose a relatively heavier burden on the groups with higher total expenditure.

The compensating and equivalent variations are shown in Table 5.4. This table also shows the values of the Frisch parameters implied by the above functional form, evaluated at the midpoints of the classes. The compensating

Table 5.4: Compensating and Equivalent Variations

m	ξ	CV	CV/m	EV	EV/m	tax
50	-20.989	2.47	0.049	2.30	0.046	2.30
60	-19.160	3.28	0.055	2.98	0.050	2.98
70	-17.739	4.56	0.065	4.10	0.059	4.10
80	-16.593	5.51	0.069	5.06	0.063	5.07
90	-15.644	6.33	0.070	5.85	0.065	5.85

variations, expressed as ratios of total expenditure, indicate that, as expected, the burden of the tax system falls more heavily on the upper income groups. The tax raised at the midpoint expenditure level is also given in the final column of the table. If a uniform indirect tax of 0.15 were imposed on each good, the ratio of the compensating variation to total expenditure would be 0.15 in each total expenditure group. The corresponding ratio of the equivalent income to total expenditure would also be the same in each total expenditure group, at 0.13; this is the value of the uniform tax expressed as a tax-inclusive rather than a tax-exclusive rate. The tax-inclusive rate corresponding to the tax-exclusive rate of t is equal to $t/(1+t)$.

A more detailed analysis of the welfare effects of the tax structure can be obtained by evaluating inequality measures and associated social welfare functions using the distribution of equivalent incomes. Consider the use of the Atkinson (1970) inequality measure, $A(\varepsilon)$, for inequality aversion coefficient ε, and, following Yitzhaki (1983), the extended Gini measure, $G(v)$, where v has a role similar to that of ε, and a value of $v = 2$ gives the standard Gini measure. The use of these inequality measures implies very different fundamental value judgements, but they are both associated with an abbreviated social welfare function of the form $\bar{m}_e(1 - I_{m_e})$, where $\bar{m}_e$ and I_{m_e} denote respectively the arithmetic mean and inequality measure based on equivalent incomes; for treatments of inequality measures and their associated abbreviated welfare functions, see Lambert (1993b) and Creedy (1996).

First, the pre-tax distribution of total expenditure can be obtained directly from the household budget survey. Suppose that there are 20 house-

Table 5.5: Distribution of Total Expenditure

ε	$\bar{m}_e\left(1 - A\left(\varepsilon\right)\right)$	$A\left(\varepsilon\right)$	v	$G\left(v\right)$	$\bar{m}_e\left(1 - G\left(v\right)\right)$
0.10	66.2026	0.0022	1.10	0.0346	64.0529
0.30	65.9083	0.0067	1.30	0.0595	62.4031
0.50	65.6149	0.0111	1.50	0.0808	60.9919
0.70	65.3226	0.0155	1.70	0.0988	59.7953
0.90	65.0317	0.0199	1.90	0.1141	58.7811
1.10	64.7425	0.0242	2.10	0.1271	57.9183
1.30	64.4553	0.0286	2.30	0.1382	57.1803
1.50	64.1701	0.0329	2.50	0.1478	56.5454

holds whose total expenditures are [45, 48, 50, 51, 53, 56, 60, 62, 63, 64, 68, 71, 74, 76, 78, 80, 84, 92, 94]. The measures of inequality and the associated welfare measures for a range of aversion coefficients, based on this distribution, are shown in Table 5.5.

The tax structure is found to give rise to a set of equivalent incomes, corresponding to the above total expenditures, of [42.93, 45.79, 47.70, 48.65, 50.56, 53.22, 55.12, 57.02, 58.92, 59.87, 60.82, 64.02, 66.85, 69.67, 71.19, 73.06, 74.94, 78.68, 86.02, 89.89]. In evaluating these equivalent incomes, each individual is first assigned to the appropriate total expenditure group, and then the corresponding set of elasticities and parameter values for that group are applied. The resulting measures are shown in Table 5.6, which may be compared with Table 5.5. The imposed tax structure is not of course revenue neutral, since no consideration has been given to the way in which the tax revenue is spent by the government. It is therefore not surprising that the values of the abbreviated welfare functions all fall. In realistic cases it is clearly important to consider the expenditure side as well as the tax side of government activity. All of the inequality measures can also be seen to fall as a result of the tax. This is not surprising in view of the simplicity of the example, and suggests that the post-tax Lorenz curve of equivalent income lies entirely inside that of the pre-tax distribution of total expenditure. In practice, it is not uncommon for the inequality measures to depend on the degree of inequality aversion, so that the Lorenz curves intersect.

Table 5.6: Equivalent Income

ε	$\bar{m}_e\left(1 - A\left(\varepsilon\right)\right)$	$A\left(\varepsilon\right)$	v	$G\left(v\right)$	$\bar{m}_e\left(1 - G\left(v\right)\right)$
0.10	62.5164	0.0021	1.10	0.0334	60.5523
0.30	62.2577	0.0062	1.30	0.0574	59.0519
0.50	61.9996	0.0103	1.50	0.0779	57.7677
0.70	61.7425	0.0144	1.70	0.0953	56.6777
0.90	61.4864	0.0185	1.90	0.1100	55.7527
1.10	61.2317	0.0226	2.10	0.1226	54.9648
1.30	60.9785	0.0266	2.30	0.1334	54.2899
1.50	60.7270	0.0306	2.50	0.1427	53.7082

5.4 Conclusions

This chapter has shown how estimates of the parameters of the linear expenditure system can be obtained for a range of different total expenditure groups using only cross-sectional budget data, and how this information can be used to calculate the compensating and equivalent variations, and the equivalent income, resulting from a tax change. Such measures can be used to examine the welfare effects of any set of price changes. The approach presented requires only proportionate price changes, rather than price levels.

These measures of welfare change can be applied to a wide variety of tax structure changes in order to determine the effect on the welfare of individuals in different income groups. Alternative social welfare functions can be used to evaluate the resulting distribution of equivalent income.

The parametric approach provides a convenient method of evaluating the effects of price changes resulting from a wide range of causes. It is particularly useful where few data are available, but of course a degree of caution should always be exercised in view of the use of strong restrictions and the need to make assumptions about the variation in the Frisch parameter. For this reason, sensitivity analyses are recommended. Examples of the use of the approach developed in this chapter are given in part III below.

Appendix: Additive Preferences

This appendix shows how the Frisch expressions for price elasticities, under additive preferences, can be derived. Consider the directly additive utility function:

$$U(x) = \sum_{k=1}^{n} U_k(x_k) \qquad (5.47)$$

which is maximised subject to the budget constraint:

$$\sum_{i=1}^{n} p_i x_i = m \qquad (5.48)$$

The Lagrangian for this problem is $U(x) + \lambda(m - \sum p_i x_i)$. Appropriate differentiation gives the usual n first-order conditions, $u_i = p_i \lambda$, where u_i is dU/dx_i. Taking logarithms of each condition gives:

$$\log u_i = \log \lambda + \log p_i \qquad (5.49)$$

Differentiating both sides of equation (5.49) with respect to $\log m$ gives:

$$\frac{\partial \log u_i}{\partial \log m} = \frac{\partial \log \lambda}{\partial \log m} \qquad (5.50)$$

Using $e_i = \partial \log x_i / \partial \log m$, this becomes:

$$\left(\frac{\partial \log u_i}{\partial \log x_i} \right) e_i = \frac{\partial \log \lambda}{\partial \log m} \qquad (5.51)$$

The Lagrangian coefficient λ is interpreted as the marginal utility of income (total expenditure). Hence, the right-hand side of equation (5.51) is the income elasticity of the marginal utility of income. It is expected to be negative in view of the concavity of the utility function. This elasticity was described by Frisch (1959, p.183) as 'the flexibility of the marginal utility of money', but is now more widely known as the 'Frisch parameter', ξ. Hence (5.51) can be rewritten as:

$$\frac{\partial \log u_i}{\partial \log x_i} = \frac{\xi}{e_i} \qquad (5.52)$$

Returning to the logarithmic form of each first-order condition in equation (5.49) and differentiating with respect to p_j gives:

$$\frac{\partial \log u_i}{\partial \log p_j} = \frac{\partial \log \lambda}{\partial \log p_j} + \frac{\partial \log p_i}{\partial \log p_j} \qquad (5.53)$$

The last term in equation (5.53) is either 1 or 0, when $i = j$ or $i \neq j$ respectively. Hence it can be written using the Kronecker delta, defined as $\delta_{ij} = 1$ if $i = j$, and $\delta_{ij} = 0$ if $i \neq j$. Furthermore, dividing throughout by the cross-price elasticity, $\eta_{ij} = \partial \log x_i / \partial \log p_j$, this becomes:

$$\frac{\partial \log u_i}{\partial \log x_i} = \frac{1}{\eta_{ij}} \left(\frac{\partial \log \lambda}{\partial \log p_j} \right) + \frac{\delta_{ij}}{\eta_{ij}} \qquad (5.54)$$

Combining (5.52) and (5.54) to eliminate $\partial \log u_i / \partial \log x_i$ gives:

$$\eta_{ij} \xi = e_i \left(\frac{\partial \log \lambda}{\partial \log p_j} \right) + e_i \delta_{ij} \qquad (5.55)$$

Multiplying both sides by the share of expenditure devoted to the ith commodity, w_i, gives:

$$\xi \eta_{ij} w_i = w_i e_i \left(\frac{\partial \log \lambda}{\partial \log p_j} \right) + w_i e_i \delta_{ij} \qquad (5.56)$$

A further simplification of equation (5.56) can be obtained using two aggregation conditions, sometimes referred to as Engel and Cournot aggregation respectively, which state that $\sum_{i=1}^{n} w_i e_i = 1$ and $\sum_{i=1}^{n} w_i \eta_{ij} = -w_j$. Both of these conditions result directly from the budget constraint $m = \sum_{i=1}^{n} p_i x_i$. In the first case differentiate the budget constraint with respect to m, giving

$\sum_{i=1}^{n} p_i(\partial x_i/\partial m) = 1$, and in the second case, differentiate it totally to give $dm = \sum_{i=1}^{n} x_i dp_i + \sum_{i=1}^{n} p_i dx_i$.

Summing (5.54) over all i and using these two aggregation conditions gives, after rearrangement:

$$\frac{\partial \log \lambda}{\partial \log p_j} = -\xi w_j - w_j e_j. \tag{5.57}$$

Using this result to substitute for $\partial \log \lambda/\partial \log p_j$ in (5.56) and rearranging yields the required expression for the price elasticities:

$$\eta_{ij} = -e_i w_j \left(1 + \frac{e_j}{\xi}\right) + \frac{e_i \delta_{ij}}{\xi} \tag{5.58}$$

These elasticity expressions automatically satisfy the homogeneity and additivity restrictions. Additive preferences can be seen to imply that all goods are net substitutes.

Chapter 6

Equivalent Incomes and Optimal Taxation

The standard approach to the analysis of optimal income taxation involves the maximisation of a social welfare function specified in terms of individuals' utilities; see, for example, Atkinson and Stiglitz (1980, pp. 405-422), Heady (1993) and Creedy (1996). Within this framework it has been found that the optimal linear income tax rate is not very sensitive to the degree of relative inequality aversion of the welfare function. It is, however, sensitive to the elasticity of substitution between leisure and consumption. Following extensive simulations, Stern (1976) suggested that the case for high optimal tax rates rests on an assumption of a low elasticity of substitution rather than a high degree of inequality aversion.

The implications of using the concept of equivalent income in optimal income tax studies in place of utilities have received little attention. Equivalent income was defined in chapters 2 and 4; it measures the income that, at some reference set of prices and wages, gives the same utility as an individual's actual income. It transforms utility into expenditure levels, and provides a particular form of indirect utility function representing the preference ordering. Welfare comparisons between different tax systems can be made for a fixed set of reference prices.

This chapter examines the implications of using individuals' equivalent incomes in place of utility, in the context of the optimal linear income tax. The choice between utility levels or equivalent incomes in the social welfare function involves a value judgement just as the form of welfare function itself obviously involves a value judgement. Hence, it is not the purpose of this chapter to argue that any particular welfare measure should be used in analyses of alternative tax structures. Rather, consistent with the general approach to optimal taxation, the analysis involves exploring the implications of adopting alternative value judgements.

A major finding is that there is less inequality in utility than in equivalent income, and the marginal social welfare from higher wage people is lower for utility compared with equivalent income. These two features have opposing effects on the optimal marginal tax. When inequality aversion is very low, the first effect is small and the optimal tax is expected to be lower when using equivalent income compared with utility. Similarly, when inequality aversion is high, the relatively higher inequality of equivalent income dominates and the associated optimal tax is expected to be higher than when utility is used. The net result is that the optimal result is expected to be more sensitive to inequality aversion when using equivalent income than when using utility in the social welfare function.

The use of utility and the relationship between alternative cardinalisations of the utility function and social welfare is discussed in section 6.1. Equivalent incomes are derived in section 6.2 and numerical examples using Cobb-Douglas utility functions are given in section 6.3. The Cobb-Douglas case has the advantage that the government's budget constraint can be solved relatively easily. The use of constant elasticity of substitution, CES, utility functions is examined in section 6.4, allowing for variations in the elasticity of substitution between leisure and consumption. The argument that the case for a high optimal rate rests on the assumption of a low elasticity of substitution rather than a high degree of inequality aversion is considered.

6.1 Cardinalisation Issues

In the standard form of the optimal linear income tax problem it is required to select the values of the social dividend, a, and constant marginal tax rate, t, in order to maximise a social welfare function W. The latter is expressed as a function of individual utilities, so that $W = W(U_1, ..., U_N)$. In a pure transfer system this must satisfy the government's budget constraint that $a = t\bar{y}$, where $\bar{y}$ is arithmetic mean earnings. At the same time each individual is maximising utility $U_i = U_i(c_i, h_i)$ where c and h respectively denote consumption (net income) and leisure, expressed as a proportion of total time available. If the price of consumption is normalised to unity and the wage obtained by person i is w_i, each individual's budget constraint is expressed as $c_i = w_i(1-t)(1-h_i) + a$. The 'dual optimisation' nature of the problem and the need to deal with corner solutions means that simulation methods have to be used in order to solve for the optimal tax rate. In view of the government's budget constraint, there is only one degree of freedom in the choice of tax parameters, so it is only necessary to search over values of the marginal tax rate, t. In specifying the extent of heterogeneity in the model, it is usual to assume that there is an exogenous distribution of wage rates, w_i, but that all individuals have the same tastes and face the same tax rates and commodity prices.

A much-used form for the social welfare function is the constant relative inequality aversion form:

$$W = \frac{1}{1-\varepsilon} \sum_i U_i^{1-\varepsilon} \qquad \text{for } \varepsilon \neq 1 \text{ and } \varepsilon > 0 \tag{6.1}$$

$$= \sum_i \log U_i \qquad \text{for } \varepsilon = 1 \tag{6.2}$$

where ε is the inequality aversion parameter. An advantage of this form is that it can easily be expressed in abbreviated form with welfare per person written as $\left\{\bar{U}(1-I)\right\}^{(1-\varepsilon)}/(1-\varepsilon)$, where $\bar{U}$ and I respectively denote arithmetic mean utility and Atkinson's inequality measure $I = 1 - U_e/\bar{U}$, with U_e as the equally distributed equivalent level of utility. However, it is more common to use the monotonic transformation:

$$W_m = \bar{U}(1-I) \tag{6.3}$$

since the trade-off between $\bar{U}$ and I is unchanged. This form of welfare function is often combined with the use of Cobb-Douglas utility functions:

$$U_i = c_i^{\alpha} h_i^{1-\alpha} \tag{6.4}$$

It is well known that the optimal tax depends on the cardinalisation of the utility function. In particular, the same consumption and labour supply is obtained for each individual using:

$$U_i' = \alpha \log c_i + (1 - \alpha) \log h_i \tag{6.5}$$

yet optimal tax rates differ. However, the combination (6.2) and (6.4) is similar to the combination of (6.1), with $\varepsilon = 0$, and (6.5). Inequality aversion of 0 and 1 can therefore give the same optimal tax rate, if particular cardinalisations of the utility function are used. This has long been recognised; see, for example, the discussion by Heady (1993). Nevertheless, it does not seem to have been regarded as a cause for concern. The remainder of this section examines this aspect in more detail.

Consider the logarithmic form of welfare function in (6.2). It can be seen that the equally distributed equivalent utility level is equal to the geometric mean utility level, U_G. Using the cardinalisation of individuals' utility functions in (6.4), abbreviated social welfare, W^*, from (6.3) is simply $\bar{U} - U_G$, or the difference between the arithmetic mean and geometric mean utility. However, for $\varepsilon = 0$, inequality is obviously zero and the equally distributed equivalent utility level is the arithmetic mean value of U', that is $\bar{U}'$.

If the cardinalisation (6.5) is used too, then $\bar{U}'$ is the logarithm of the geometric mean, U_G, so the corresponding abbreviated social welfare, W', is $\log U_G$. The relationship between the two abbreviated values of social welfare is thus:

$$W' = \log \left(\bar{U} - W^* \right) \tag{6.6}$$

There is a further aspect of the cardinalisation that does not seem to be so widely recognised. The addition of a constant term to the utility function (6.4), or indeed to (6.5), clearly has no effect on each individual's consumption and labour supply. Suppose that a fixed amount, θ, is added to each individual's utility, U_i. This means that, instead of maximising (6.1) or (6.2), the welfare function, W_θ, is maximised, where:

$$W_\theta = \frac{1}{1-\varepsilon} \sum_i (U_i + \theta)^{1-\varepsilon} \text{ for } \varepsilon \neq 1 \text{ and } \varepsilon \geq 0 \tag{6.7}$$

$$= \sum_i \log (U_i + \theta) \text{ for } \varepsilon = 1 \tag{6.8}$$

The addition of a constant to each person's utility, with (6.1) or (6.2), is therefore equivalent to retaining the original cardinalisation, as in (6.4), but adopting a social welfare function that no longer reflects constant relative inequality aversion. From (6.7), for example, the relative inequality aversion is given, where $H(U_i) = (U_i + \theta)^{1-\varepsilon} / (1 - \varepsilon)$, by:

$$\frac{-U_i H''(U_i)}{H'(U_i) + \theta} = \frac{\varepsilon U_i}{U_i + \theta} \tag{6.9}$$

and is not constant. Furthermore, the absolute inequality aversion is given by:

$$\frac{-H''(U_i)}{H'(U_i)} = \frac{\varepsilon}{U_i + \theta} \tag{6.10}$$

The form of the welfare function in (6.7) may be said to reflect constant 'intermediate' aversion to inequality. The marginal rate of substitution between U_i and U_j along a social indifference curve showing combinations of U_i and U_j for which W_θ is constant, is given by:

$$-\frac{dU_i}{dU_j}\bigg|_{W_\theta} = \left(\frac{U_i + \theta}{U_j + \theta}\right)^\varepsilon \tag{6.11}$$

This is constant for a constant value of the ratio $(U_i + \theta) / (U_j + \theta)$. This contrasts with constant relative aversion where the marginal rate of substitution is constant for a fixed ratio of U_i/U_j, and constant absolute aversion where the marginal rate of substitution is constant for a fixed absolute difference between the two utilities. On the use of this type of welfare function, see Kolm (1976), along with Pfingsten (1987) and Besley and Preston (1988).

6.2   Equivalent Incomes

These difficulties associated with alternative cardinalisations of utility functions suggest that it may be of interest to examine the use of a social welfare
function which is expressed in terms of a money metric welfare measure.
Consider, then, the use of equivalent income; that is, the level of equivalent
income is substituted for the utility level of each individual in the social welfare function. This is defined as the value of income that, at some reference
set of prices, p_r, gives the same utility as the actual income. This represents a transformation of utility into expenditure levels, and is not subject
to cardinalisation difficulties; see also chapter 4 above.

In general, where the direct utility function is written as $U = U(x)$,
where x is a vector of consumption levels, and the indirect form is written
as $V = V(p, m)$, where m is income (the budget) and p is a vector of prices,
equivalent income, m_e, is defined by:

$$V(p_r, m_e) = V(p, m) \tag{6.12}$$

The expenditure or cost function $E(p, U)$, gives the minimum expenditure required to achieve utility level U at prices, p; see chapters 2 and 4. Equivalent
income can therefore be expressed as:

$$m_e = E(p_r, V(p, m)) \tag{6.13}$$

In the standard two-good Cobb-Douglas case of consumption of x_1, and of
x_2 of the goods at given prices p_1 and p_2 respectively, $U(x) = x_1^\alpha x_2^{1-\alpha}$ and
the indirect utility function is:

$$V(p, m) = m \left(\frac{\alpha}{p_1}\right)^\alpha \left(\frac{1-\alpha}{p_2}\right)^{1-\alpha} \tag{6.14}$$

Hence the expenditure function is given by:

$$E(p, U) = U \left(\frac{p_1}{\alpha}\right)^\alpha \left(\frac{p_2}{1-\alpha}\right)^{1-\alpha} \tag{6.15}$$

By substituting the right-hand side of (6.14) for U in the expenditure function, the income, m_e, needed to achieve U at the set of references prices, p_r, is given by:

$$m_e = m \left(\frac{p_{r1}}{p_1}\right)^{\alpha} \left(\frac{p_{r2}}{p_1}\right)^{1-\alpha} \tag{6.16}$$

A feature of the equivalent income function is that cardinalisation difficulties do not arise because it is invariant with respect to monotonic transformations of the utility function; it represents a particular monotonic transformation of utility, for given reference prices.

In the present context of labour supply variations one of the goods is consumption while the other is leisure. Income is not exogenously given but depends on labour supply. However, the above results can be applied directly by replacing income, m, with 'full income', given in the present case of a linear tax by $M = w(1 - t) + a$; this represents the maximum income, obtained by devoting all available time to work and consuming no leisure. The price of leisure is $w(1 - t)$, while the price of consumption remains fixed at unity. Suppose that the reference prices are those that are relevant in the situation where there is no tax, so that $a = t = 0$ and full income is simply the wage rate, w. When $t > 0$, the value of equivalent income for the Cobb-Douglas case is given by substituting into (6.16), so that:

$$m_e = \{w(1 - t) + a\} \left(\frac{1}{1 - t}\right)^{1-\alpha} \tag{6.17}$$

This result applies for tangency solutions, that is, for those who work. Those who do not work and for whom $h = 1$ receive only the unconditional transfer, a, so that the full income required to achieve utility of a^{α} at the reference prices is given by:

$$m_e = a^{\alpha} \left(\frac{1}{\alpha}\right)^{\alpha} \left(\frac{w}{1 - \alpha}\right)^{1-\alpha} \tag{6.18}$$

This value applies for $w \leq a (1 - \alpha) / \{\alpha (1 - t)\} = w_L$.

This chapter thus investigates the effect of substituting m_e for U, for each individual, in the social welfare function. Some idea of the possible difference between the use of equivalent incomes and utility can be obtained by comparing (6.17) with utility. Appropriate substitution into the indirect form of the utility function in (6.14) gives an expression that is the same as (6.17) but is multiplied by $\alpha^\alpha (1 - \alpha)^{1-\alpha} w^{-(1-\alpha)}$. The proportional term involving α is unimportant, but the term involving w means that there is less inequality in utility than in equivalent income, and the marginal social welfare from higher wage people is lower for utility compared with equivalent income. These two features have opposing effects on the optimal marginal tax rate. When inequality aversion is very low, the first effect is small and the optimal tax is expected to be lower when using equivalent income compared with utility. Similarly, when inequality aversion is high, the relatively higher inequality of equivalent income dominates and the associated optimal tax is expected to be higher than when utility is used. It can be shown that the profiles of the optimal tax rate plotted against inequality aversion must intersect when $\varepsilon = 1$. This is because, in this case, the difference between $\sum \log m_e$ and $\sum \log V$ does not depend on t. Hence the value of t for which these two objectives reach a maximum is the same for both.

6.3 Numerical Examples

Comparisons of the implications of using alternative cardinalisations of the utility function and using equivalent income can be made using simulation methods. Suppose that wage rates follow the lognormal distribution with variance of logarithms of 0.5. Furthermore, assume that $\alpha = 0.6$. The first step is to solve for a, given values of t, using the government's budget constraint, $a = t\bar{m}$, for a pure transfer scheme. Since $\bar{m}$ depends on the transfer, a, this constraint must be solved iteratively using the result that:

$$\bar{m} = \alpha \bar{w} G_\gamma (w_L) \tag{6.19}$$

where $\bar{w}$ is the arithmetic mean wage rate and:

$$G_\xi (w_L) = \{1 - F_1 (w_L)\} - \left(\frac{\gamma}{\alpha \bar{w}}\right) \{1 - F (w_L)\} \tag{6.20}$$

Table 6.1: Optimum Tax Rates

ε	Optimum Tax Rate Using:			
	U	$logU$	$100+U$	m_e
0	0.305	0.410	0.305	0.005
0.2	0.335	0.410	0.320	0.170
0.4	0.355	0.415	0.330	0.260
0.6	0.375	0.420	0.345	0.325
0.8	0.405	0.420	0.350	0.375
1.0	0.410	0.425	0.360	0.410
1.2	0.420	0.430	0.370	0.440
1.4	0.430	0.430	0.380	0.460
1.6	0.440	0.430	0.380	0.480
10.0	0.570	0.500	0.635	0.635

$F(w)$ is the distribution function and $F_1(w)$ is the first moment distribution defined by $F_1(w) = \int_0^w u dF(u)/\bar{w}$. For those who work, earnings are given by $m = \alpha w - \gamma$, with $\gamma = a(1-\alpha)/(1-t)$; for further details, see Creedy (1994).

A simulated population of 5000 individuals was generated in order to calculate the optimum tax rates shown in Table 6.1. In each case, the value of t was varied in steps of 0.005, and a grid search was carried out. The optimal tax rate is reported for variations in values of the relative inequality aversion parameter, ε. For infinitely large ε, the solution approaches the maxi-min, which maximises the welfare associated with the poorest person, so that in each case the optimum marginal rate approaches the value that maximises the threshold, a. This rate is found to be given by $t = 0.64$.

Table 6.1 shows, as expected, that the optimal tax rate with $\log U$ and $\varepsilon = 0$ is the same as with U and $\varepsilon = 1$. The utility-based optimal rates show substantially less variation with ε and approach the maxi-min value more slowly, compared with the use of equivalent income. For example, when ε reaches 1.4, the optimal rates using U and $\log U$ are equal (the profiles of optimal t against ε intersect at this point). The difference between results for U and $100 + U$ can, as suggested above, be interpreted in terms of the difference between the use of constant relative and 'intermediate' inequality aversion. The profiles of optimal t against ε, for U and m_e, cross where $\varepsilon = 1$; this reflects the general result discussed in the previous section.

6.4 CES Utility Functions

This section relaxes the assumption of a unitary elasticity of substitution between leisure and consumption, and uses the CES specification of the utility function for each individual. This allows results to be compared with those of Stern (1976). The first two subsections derive equivalent income in the general case and for the linear tax involving labour supply variations respectively. Numerical examples are then reported for a variety of simulations.

6.4.1 The General Case

In general, with goods $x_1...x_k$, the CES utility function is written as:

$$U(x) = \left(\sum_{i=1}^{k} \beta_i x_i^\rho \right)^{-1/\rho} \tag{6.21}$$

with $\beta_i > 0$. The elasticity of substitution between all pairs of goods is given by $\sigma = 1/(1+\rho)$. If (6.21) is maximised subject to the budget constraint $m = \sum x_i p_i$, the following demand functions are obtained:

$$x_i = m\Psi \left(\frac{\beta_i}{p_i} \right)^\sigma \tag{6.22}$$

where:

$$\Psi = \left[\sum_{i=1}^{k} p_i \left(\frac{\beta_i}{p_i} \right)^\sigma \right]^{-1} \tag{6.23}$$

Hence the indirect utility function is given by:

$$\begin{aligned} V(p,m) &= m\Psi \left[\sum \beta_i \left(\frac{\beta_i}{p_i} \right)^{-\rho\sigma} \right]^{-1/\rho} \\ &= m\Psi\Phi \end{aligned} \tag{6.24}$$

and the expenditure function is:

$$E\left(p, U\right) = \left(\Psi\Phi\right)^{-1} U \tag{6.25}$$

Using the subscript r to denote evaluation of the terms Ψ and Φ at references prices, equivalent income, m_e, is given by:

$$m_e = m\left(\frac{\Psi\Phi}{\Psi_r\Phi_r}\right) \tag{6.26}$$

6.4.2 Labour Supply

If good 1 is consumption, with $p_1 = 1$, and good 2 is leisure, with a price of $p_2 = w(1-t)$, m must be replaced by full income $M = a + w(1-t)$ for the linear income tax. Furthermore, let $\beta_1 = \alpha$ and $\beta_2 = 1 - \alpha$. Hence substitution into (6.23) and (6.24) gives:

$$\Psi = \left[a^\sigma + w(1-t)\left\{\frac{1-\alpha}{w\left(1-t\right)}\right\}^\sigma\right]^{-1} \tag{6.27}$$

$$\Phi = \left[\alpha\alpha^{-\rho\sigma} + (1-\alpha)\left\{\frac{1-\alpha}{w\left(1-t\right)}\right\}^{-\rho\sigma}\right]^{-1/\rho} \tag{6.28}$$

If the reference set of prices is the no-tax case where $t = a = 0$, the value of equivalent income can be obtained by direct substitution into (6.26). However, this expression applies to tangency solutions where $h < 1$, which requires w to exceed a minimum value w_L. From (6.22), suitably modified, the consumption of leisure, h, is given by:

$$h = \Psi M\left\{\frac{1-\alpha}{w\left(1-t\right)}\right\}^\sigma \tag{6.29}$$

with Ψ given by (6.27). Thus it can be found that $h = 1$ when:

$$w_L = \frac{\alpha^{1/\sigma}}{1-t}\left(\frac{1-\alpha}{\alpha}\right) \tag{6.30}$$

When $w < w_L$, only the transfer payment, a, is available for consumption and, with $h = 1$, utility is:

$$U = \left[\alpha a^{-\rho} + (1 - \alpha) \right]^{-1/\rho} \tag{6.31}$$

Substituting (6.31) into the expenditure function (6.25), for reference prices, gives equivalent income of:

$$m_e = \left\{ \alpha a^{-\rho} + (1 - \alpha) \right\}^{-1/\rho} (\Psi_r \Phi_r)^{-1} \tag{6.32}$$

where Ψ_r and Φ_r are obtained from (6.27) and (6.28) by substituting $t = 0$. The CES case is therefore more cumbersome than the use of Cobb-Douglas utility functions, but involves no new basic principles. However, it is not possible to obtain convenient expressions corresponding to (6.19) and (6.20) for the government's budget constraint. This is because of the non-linearity in the relationship between earnings and the wage rate for each individual. This means that in examining numerical results it is necessary to solve the budget constraint iteratively using the simulated values for all individuals and aggregating.

6.4.3   Numerical Examples

Care must be taken in calibrating the CES case, particularly concerning the choice of values of α and σ. When $\sigma < 1$ the labour supply curve, unlike the Cobb-Douglas case, can be 'backward bending'. Empirical work suggests that the elasticity of substitution is less than one. In the above example involving Cobb-Douglas utility functions, the value of $\alpha = 0.6$ implies that in the absence of taxes, all individuals spend 60 per cent of their time working. For comparability, it is convenient to set α in the CES case, for a given σ, such that an individual at the arithmetic mean wage also spends 60 per cent of time in work in the absence of taxes and transfers. Suppose that $\sigma = 0.7$ and, as before, that $\sigma_w^2 = 0.5$. In the present context it is necessary to be explicit about the choice of mean-log-wage rate, μ_w. Suppose that $\mu_w = 8$, which gives rise to an arithmetic mean wage of 3827.63. The value of α of 0.9839 is found to ensure that when $w = 3830$ and $a = t = 0$, the individual works 60 per cent of the time. The CES case allows a higher transfer payment to be financed as a result of the lower impact of taxation on labour supply.

Table 6.2: Optimum Tax Rates with CES

	Based on:	
ε	U	m_e
0	0.34	0.005
0.2	0.38	0.2
0.4	0.41	0.3
0.6	0.43	0.38
0.8	0.45	0.43
1.0	0.46	0.46
1.2	0.48	0.5
1.4	0.49	0.52
1.6	0.5	0.54
10.0	0.64	0.71

For a pure transfer system examined here, it is known from Stern (1976) that the optimal tax rate increases as the elasticity of substitution falls and becomes 100 per cent for $\sigma = 0$.

The optimal tax rates for social welfare functions specified in terms of utility, using the usual cardinalisation of (6.21), and equivalent income, are shown in Table 6.2 for a range of inequality aversion parameters. In producing these values, $N = 2,000$; t was varied in steps of 0.01; $\sigma_w^2 = 0.5$; $\mu_w = 8.0$; $\sigma = 0.7$; $\alpha = 0.9839$. These results can be compared with Table 6.1. Again the profiles of optimal t against ε intersect at the point where $\varepsilon = 1$. As with the Cobb-Douglas case, the optimal tax rate when using U shows very little variation over a wide range of values of ε, and is very slow to approach its maxi-min rate, in view of the fact that $\varepsilon = 10.0$ may for practical purposes be regarded as extremely high. As Stern suggested, 'an argument for very high rates (say above 70%) must be based (if it is rooted in our model) on a claim that $[\sigma]$ is very low (say less than 0.1 or 0.2) rather than an extreme view of values [of ε] or the government revenue requirement' (1976, p.154). However, as Table 6.2 shows, high inequality aversion with σ of 0.7 is capable of producing a high optimal rate when equivalent income is used.

It is of interest to consider the effect of reducing the elasticity of substitution. Table 6.3 shows optimal rates for a lower value of σ of 0.6, for two

Table 6.3: Optimum Tax Rates: CES Utility $\sigma = 0.6$

	$\alpha = 0.9839$		$\alpha = 0.9979$	
ε	U	m_e	U	m_e
0	0.38	-	0.37	-
0.2	0.39	0.14	0.40	0.21
0.4	0.40	0.24	0.44	0.32
0.6	0.41	0.32	0.46	0.40
0.8	0.42	0.38	0.48	0.45
1.0	0.43	0.43	0.49	0.50
1.2	0.44	0.47	0.51	0.53
1.4	0.45	0.50	0.52	0.55
1.6	0.46	0.53	0.53	0.57
10.0	0.58	0.70	0.67	0.74

values of α. The first value is the same as used in Table 6.2. It should be recognised that variation in σ, with α unchanged, implies a different 'base' level of leisure in the no-tax case. Thus the combination of $\alpha = 0.9839$ and $\sigma = 0.6$ implies, at the wage of 3830, 30 per cent of the time being spent in work (compared with 60 per cent for the case where $\sigma = 0.7$). Comparisons which hold this base level of leisure constant require α to be increased to 0.9979 when σ is reduced to 0.6. In the first case, the lower labour supply implies a lower transfer payment for each tax rate and slightly lower optimal tax rates. When α is adjusted appropriately, the reduction in σ leads to higher optimal rates, as shown in Table 6.3. As before, the optimal rate corresponding to the use of equivalent income in the social welfare function increases with ε more rapidly than when utility is used.

6.5 Conclusions

This chapter has compared the use of equivalent incomes and utility in the social welfare function, in the determination of the optimal linear income tax rate. Equivalent income is a money metric welfare measure as it transforms utility into expenditure levels. It thus represents a particular form of indirect utility function representing the preference ordering. It is not affected by monotonic transformations of the utility function. The object of the exercise was to compare results using alternative measures, not to recommend any particular measure. Indeed, as stressed by Ebert (1995, p.295), 'it makes no sense to seek *"the* correct welfare measure"'.

It was found that the use of equivalent incomes in a social welfare function produces an optimal linear income tax rate that is more sensitive to the degree of inequality aversion than when utility is used. With the multiplicative form of the Cobb-Douglas utility function and the CES utility function, the optimal tax rate is the same for utility and equivalent income for the special case of $\varepsilon = 1$. Unlike the use of utility, it was found that with equivalent incomes the case for high marginal rates does not depend on assumption of a very low elasticity of substitution between consumption and leisure.

Part III

Applications

Chapter 7

Marginal Tax Reform

The calculation of optimal indirect tax rates requires a great deal of information about preferences and demand patterns, which is extremely difficult to obtain even in countries with rich data sources. One response to this problem is to concentrate instead on marginal tax reform, following the type of approach discussed in chapter 3, and developed by Ahmad and Stern (1984, 1991). They examined indirect tax reform by extending an approach, introduced by Feldstein (1972), which allows the same sort of distributional weights as used in optimal tax calculations to be imposed. As in the standard optimal tax approach, the method considers the implications of adopting a social welfare function specified in terms of individuals' utilities.

This chapter uses the Ahmad and Stern approach to examine marginal indirect tax reform in Australia. A special problem is raised because of the fact that there is a large variety of different types of indirect tax. They include payroll tax, fringe benefits tax, taxes on property (including financial transactions), sales taxes, excises and levies, taxes on international trade, taxes on gambling and insurance, motor vehicle and franchise taxes; see, for example, Johnson *et al.* (1997). The evaluation of the effect of these taxes on final consumers is extremely complex, involving the appropriate allowance for inter-industry transactions. This chapter uses a set of effective rates reported by Scutella (1997), who used a method based on that of Chisholm (1993).

Section 7.1 describes the basic approach used. Section 7.2 explains how the various components of the model are obtained for Australia, and section

7.3 presents empirical results.

7.1   Marginal Revenue Costs

Let V_h denote the indirect utility of the hth household, for $h = 1, ..., H$. The social welfare function, W, which represents the value judgements of a decision-maker or judge, can be expressed in general terms as the individualistic function $W = W(V_1, ..., V_H)$. Instead of attempting to find the tax structure that maximises W, Ahmad and Stern (1984) considered changes in W produced by small changes in prices. Differentiating with respect to the price of the ith good, p_i, gives:

$$\frac{\partial W}{\partial p_i} = \sum_{h=1}^{H} \frac{\partial W}{\partial V_h} \frac{\partial V_h}{\partial p_i} \tag{7.1}$$

Use can then be made of Roy's identity (the envelope theorem) which establishes a link between the Marshallian demands, $x_{hi}(p, m_h)$, where m_h is total household expenditure, and the indirect utility function, such that:

$$x_{hi}(p, m_h) = -\frac{\partial V_h(p, m_h)/\partial p_i}{\partial V_h(p, m_h)/\partial m_h} \tag{7.2}$$

Hence:

$$\frac{\partial W}{\partial p_i} = -\sum_{h=1}^{H} v_h x_{hi} \tag{7.3}$$

with:

$$v_h = \frac{\partial W}{\partial V_h} \frac{\partial V_h}{\partial m_h} \tag{7.4}$$

The term v_h is the social marginal utility of income (total expenditure) of household h.

In the context of tax reform, the price changes arise from changes in indirect taxes, which are assumed to be fully passed on to consumers, allowing for the inter-industry transactions involved before goods reach final consumers. Hence, if p_i is the post-tax price and t_i is the tax imposed on each unit of good i, then $\partial p_i = \partial t_i$.

The aggregate tax revenue from taxes on all n goods, R, is given by:

$$R = \sum_{h=1}^{H} \sum_{k=1}^{n} t_k x_{hk} \tag{7.5}$$

and the change in revenue arising from a change in the tax on the ith good is:

$$\frac{\partial R}{\partial t_i} = \sum_{h=1}^{H} x_{hi} + \sum_{h=1}^{H} \sum_{k=1}^{n} t_k \frac{\partial x_{hk}}{\partial p_i} \tag{7.6}$$

The ratio $(\partial W/\partial t_i)/(\partial R/\partial t_i)$ measures the reduction in social welfare per dollar of extra tax revenue resulting from a marginal increase in the tax t_i. For an optimal tax system, this ratio must be equal for all goods. In order to avoid a discontinuity if the change in revenue is zero, Madden (1995) suggested taking the reciprocal of the absolute value, giving the marginal revenue cost, MRC, of reform, ρ_i, where:

$$\rho_i = -\frac{\partial R/\partial t_i}{\partial W/\partial t_i} \tag{7.7}$$

The direction of tax reform is indicated by the relative magnitudes of this ratio for each commodity group; the rule for optimal tax reform is therefore to lower t_i relative to t_j if ρ_i is less than ρ_j.

Multiplying numerator and denominator of ρ_i by p_i gives a more convenient expression involving expenditures (rather than quantities) and cross-price elasticities, as:

$$\rho_i = \frac{\sum_{h=1}^{H} p_i x_{hi} + \sum_{h=1}^{H} \sum_{k=1}^{n} \tau_k \eta_{hki} p_k x_{hk}}{\sum_{h=1}^{H} v_h p_i x_{hi}} \tag{7.8}$$

where η_{hki} is household h's elasticity of demand for good k with respect to the price of good i, and τ_k is the ratio of the tax to the tax-inclusive price. Hence τ_i is the tax-inclusive *ad valorem* rate. It is possible to rewrite (7.8) in terms of the aggregate demand for good i, X_i. The change in revenue is $p_i X_i + \sum_k \tau_k \eta_{ki} p_k X_k$, where η_{ki} is the aggregate cross-price elasticity. Although this aggregative form is usually used, the disaggregated version is retained here in order to allow the elasticities to differ across households. A

useful property of (7.8) is that it involves changes in demand evaluated at
the current position, or first derivatives of the demand functions. This gives
a considerable reduction in the information required, compared with optimal
tax calculations.

7.2   Components of the MRC

The expression for ρ_i in (7.8) looks simple compared with the requirements
of optimal tax calculations, but it cannot be applied easily to actual tax
structures. The three components, that is, the tax rates, demand elasticities
and welfare weights, are discussed in this section.

7.2.1   Tax Rates

Indirect taxes in Australia consist of an extremely complex set which use
different tax bases. This chapter uses a set of effective tax rates imposed
on final consumers, allowing for all the inter-industry transactions involved,
that were computed by Scutella (1997). These rates were obtained for the
113 categories in the Australian input-output matrix, assuming that the indirect taxes are passed forward. However, the commodity groups used in the
input-output matrix are very different from those employed by the Household
Expenditure Survey, which provides information about household demand
changes. In particular, the Household Expenditure Survey groups goods into
only 16 classes, so that any reconciliation between the categories must necessarily be approximate.

Table 7.1 gives the Household Expenditure Survey categories along with
the effective tax rates used in this study. The table gives the values of t_i^*,
which are the effective tax-exclusive *ad valorem* rates taken from Scutella
(1997), along with the corresponding values of τ_i for each commodity group.
The required values of τ_i are tax-inclusive rates, so the relationship between
the two is given by $\tau_i = t_i^* / (1 + t_i^*)$.

Table 7.1: Effective Indirect Tax Rates

No.	Description	t^*	τ
1	Current housing costs	0	0
2	Electricity, gas and other fuels	0.1006	0.0914
3	Food and beverages	0.1226	0.1092
4	Spirits, beer and wine	0.3983	0.2848
5	Tobacco	2.2552	0.6928
6	Clothing and footwear	0.0542	0.0514
7	Furniture and appliances	0.1357	0.1195
8	Postal and telephone charges	0.0883	0.0811
9	Health services	0.0544	0.0516
10	Motor vehicles and parts	0.3210	0.2430
11	Recreational items	0.1530	0.1327
12	Personal care products	0.1407	0.1233
13	Miscellaneous	0.1448	0.1265
14	Mortgage repayments	0	0
15	House building payments	0.1990	0.1660
16	Superannuation	0	0

7.2.2 Demand Elasticities

The required set of price elasticities was obtained using a result established by Frisch (1959) for directly additive utility functions, following the approach described in chapter 5. The expressions require the use of the elasticity of the marginal utility of total expenditure with respect to total expenditure, ξ, referred to as the 'Frisch parameter'. If δ_{ij} denotes the Kroneker delta, such that $\delta_{ij} = 0$ when $i \neq j$, and $\delta_{ij} = 1$ when $i = j$, Frisch showed that if e_i denotes the total expenditure (income) elasticity of demand, the price elasticities, η_{ij}, can be written as:

$$\eta_{ij} = -e_i w_j \left(1 + \frac{e_j}{\xi}\right) + \frac{e_i \delta_{ij}}{\xi} \qquad (7.9)$$

where w_i is the budget share of good i. This ensures that all additivity and homogeneity restrictions are satisfied.

The approach used here involves evaluating a complete set of price elasticities for each of a range of M total expenditure groups. Hence an additional subscript needs to be added to the η_{ij}, w_i and e_i, and a subscript has to be added to ξ. The Household Expenditure data can be used to obtain, for each total expenditure group, the budget shares or expenditure weights, w_{ik}, for each commodity group $(i = 1, ..., n)$ and total expenditure group $(k = 1, ..., M)$. These weights can be used to find the total expenditure elasticities for each group; for further discussion of this approach in examining the welfare effects of tax changes, see chapter 5.

The raw budget shares cannot be used because they would give rise to numerous negative income elasticities. It is necessary first to obtain a smooth relationship between the weights and total expenditure. This was carried out by using the M observations for each commodity group to estimate:

$$w_{ik} = a_i + b_i \log(m_k) + c(1/m_k) \tag{7.10}$$

where m_k represents average total expenditure of households in the kth total expenditure group; for further discussion of this type of function to describe budget shares, see Deaton and Muellbauer (1980). The estimated values from the fitted regression lines were used to calculate the income elasticities in each total expenditure group. Having calculated the e_is for each total expenditure group, the required set of own- and cross-price elasticities were obtained using the above Frisch result.

A further problem is that in using (7.9) it is required to have values of the Frisch parameter, ξ_k, for each of the M total expenditure groups. This information cannot be obtained from the budget data, so it is necessary to specify a pattern using *a priori* assumptions. The linear expenditure system involves a minimum absolute value of unity, but the absolute value is likely to be relatively higher for lower income groups, for whom committed expenditure is a higher proportion of income. Some information about the variation in ξ may be obtained from studies such as Lluch *et al.* (1977) and Williams (1978) discussed in chapter 5. Based on these studies and Frisch's own conjectures, the following specification has been found to be useful for the variation in ξ with m:

$$\log(-\xi_k) = a - \alpha \log(m_k + \theta) \tag{7.11}$$

Suitable parameter values were obtained by experimenting with a range of alternatives. As a starting point, values of ξ_k corresponding to various values of m_k, conforming with *a priori* beliefs based on the studies mentioned above, were used to estimate the parameters of (7.11) using an iterative method based on maximum likelihood. Using $a = 15.2$, $\alpha = 1.227$ and $\theta = 8595$, where m_k is measured in cents per week, gives values of ξ_k ranging from about -25 for the lowest income group to -3 for the highest income group. Sensitivity analyses were carried out by investigating the effects of different parameter values for the specification in (7.11), but the results were not significantly affected.

In using this approach, households in the 1989 Household Expenditure Survey were divided into 29 total expenditure groups, giving a total of 7,424 price elasticities. When evaluating the value of ρ for each commodity group, each household in the HES was first assigned to the appropriate total expenditure group from which the corresponding elasticities were taken.

7.2.3 The Welfare Weights

It is possible to use the above approach to examine the implications of using any type of social welfare function. The usual approach is to specify the social welfare function in terms of each household's total expenditure, rather than utility: the conditions under which this is consistent are discussed by Banks *et al.* (1996). Indeed, if equivalent income is used instead of utility and if current prices are regarded as reference prices, it can be seen that v_h becomes $\partial W / \partial m_h$.

Using the constant inequality aversion form of the welfare function, the contribution to social welfare of the hth household is $m_h^{1-\varepsilon} / (1 - \varepsilon)$, where ε is the constant relative inequality aversion coefficient. This gives:

$$v_h = m_h^{-\varepsilon} \tag{7.12}$$

The implications of adopting alternative values of ε can therefore easily be examined using this framework. In practice, v_h was calculated as $(m_h/10,000)^{-\varepsilon}$, where m is, as above, weekly total expenditure in cents. The adjustment af-

Table 7.2: Marginal Indirect Tax Reform

	$\varepsilon = 0$		$\varepsilon = 0.3$				$\varepsilon = 1.2$			
no.	ρ	r_ρ	d	r_d	ρ	r_ρ	d	r_d	ρ	r_ρ
1	0.8894	14	1.6483	6	1.4661	9	5.8873	2	5.2363	5
2	0.8732	10	1.5812	1	1.3807	2	4.8612	5	4.2449	1
3	0.8730	9	1.6319	8	1.4245	4	5.6297	8	4.9145	4
4	0.8388	3	1.6896	4	1.4173	3	6.6817	3	5.6048	8
5	0.8277	1	1.6101	5	1.3326	1	5.4136	1	4.4807	2
6	0.8893	13	1.7157	7	1.5257	12	7.1105	9	6.3232	11
7	0.8727	8	1.7528	12	1.5297	13	7.7791	12	6.7889	13
8	0.8770	11	1.6280	2	1.4277	5	5.4842	4	4.8095	3
9	0.8817	12	1.6546	3	1.4589	8	6.0332	13	5.3196	7
10	0.8381	2	1.7305	15	1.4503	7	7.3967	11	6.1990	10
11	0.8688	5	1.7160	11	1.4909	10	7.0741	6	6.1461	9
12	0.8710	7	1.6582	9	1.4443	6	6.0542	10	5.2732	6
13	0.8704	6	1.7387	10	1.5134	11	7.5123	7	6.5388	12
14	0.9040	15	1.7426	16	1.5752	15	7.8775	16	7.1209	15
15	0.8466	4	1.9057	13	1.6134	16	11.8773	14	10.0554	16
16	0.9041	16	1.7411	14	1.5741	14	7.8262	15	7.0754	14

fects the absolute values of ρ, but only their relative values are of significance in considering marginal tax reform. Allowance may also be made for differences in household size, but this has been found in previous studies to have little effect and is not used here.

7.3 Empirical Results

The marginal revenue costs for the 16 Household Expenditure Survey commodity categories, using 7191 households from the 1989 survey, are given in Table 7.2 for several values of inequality aversion. The table also gives the values of the marginal revenue cost, d_i, for each good obtained by ignoring the efficiency effects of the marginal tax changes. Thus each d_i is defined as the corresponding values of ρ_i, obtained by setting all the price elasticities equal to zero. This means that when $\varepsilon = 0$, each value of d_i is equal to unity.

Since only the relative values of the ρ_is are important, Table 7.2 also gives the rankings, r_ρ, from lowest to highest values. There are some interesting changes in the rankings as ε is increased from a zero level to a positive level. When inequality aversion is absent, the results suggest raising the effective tax rate on, for example, current housing costs (at present untaxed), electricity, gas and other fuels, food and health services (commodity group numbers 1, 2, 3 and 9). However, a judge with inequality aversion would lower these tax rates; the values of the marginal revenue cost drop below the median for non-zero values of ε. These findings are not entirely surprising in view of the fact that the budget shares of these commodity groups are known to be systematically higher in the lower-income groups.

For judges with $\varepsilon = 0$, the results suggest lowering the effective indirect tax rate on motor vehicles and parts, recreational items and house building payments (commodity group numbers 10, 11 and 15). However, those with non-zero values of ε would raise the rates. Again, these results may be expected from what is known about budget shares; these items form a systematically higher proportion of the budgets of higher-income groups. Decision-makers with no aversion to inequality would disagree with those with some aversion over the appropriate pattern of marginal tax reforms.

However, in moving from $\varepsilon = 0.3$ to $\varepsilon = 1.2$, there are very few changes in the rankings, and only two categories (commodity groups 1 and 4) show any significant changes; the rank for group 1 moves across the median value and group 4 moves to the median. It can be seen that these rankings change in important ways as ε is increased from a zero to a positive value. However, increasing ε to 1.5 produced no further rank-order changes. Hence, there is a considerable agreement about the *direction* of marginal tax changes among all judges who have some aversion to inequality. The results suggest reductions in taxes for fuel and power, spirits, beer and wine, and tobacco, though there are other well-known reasons for the imposition of taxes on these commodity groups.

Unlike the finding reported by Madden (1995, p.29), there is a large degree of agreement between the rankings obtained using d_i and ρ_i, though there are some interesting exceptions. Hence, marginal reforms cannot be said to be dominated by 'efficiency' considerations.

7.4   Conclusions

This chapter has examined indirect tax reform in Australia using the method developed by Ahmad and Stern (1984). This method has the advantage of requiring less information than is needed for the calculation of optimal tax rates. Nevertheless, the application of the approach presents substantial data problems. In applying the method it is usual, in calculating the required demand changes, to use aggregate own- and cross-price demand elasticities. However, the present chapter used an approach in which the demand elasticities are allowed to vary with the value of total expenditure of the household. The effective indirect tax rates imposed on final consumers that were used in this study were taken from Scutella (1997), which allowed for the complicated inter-industry transactions involved.

In view of the problems of calculating the required tax rates for the very broad commodity groups used and the assumption of additivity, the results should be treated with caution. Furthermore, no allowance has been made for general equilibrium effects in calculating effective tax rates and full shifting has been assumed. Perhaps the most noteworthy result is the finding that the directions of optimal marginal changes efficiency are significantly affected by the existence of inequality aversion, but the degree of aversion beyond a low level has a negligible effect on the rankings

In practice, many indirect tax changes are non-marginal. This is particularly true of a major reform to indirect taxes such as a change in the direct/indirect tax mix or, for example, the replacement of a set of wholesale taxes by a general consumption tax. Such a non-marginal change is considered in the next chapter.

Chapter 8

Indirect Tax Reform

This chapter examines the welfare changes imposed on different income (total expenditure) groups by changes in prices which arise from non-marginal changes in indirect taxes. The approach is based on the use of the linear expenditure system, as described in chapter 5. The method is used to examine the distributional effects of the change in the indirect tax system in New Zealand during the mid-1980s, carried out as part of a major package of tax reforms involving a flattening of the income tax structure, a large amount of base-broadening and a partial shift towards indirect taxation. For broad descriptions of the reforms, see Stephens (1993) and St John (1993). The focus of the present chapter is very narrow since it ignores the direct tax and transfer changes and concentrates exclusively on the replacement of a range of wholesale sales taxes with a goods and services tax, the GST. However, the GST warrants close examination in view of the continued debate in New Zealand and in countries such as Australia which are considering indirect tax reforms. Indeed, Due (1988, p. 129) has suggested that 'New Zealand's Goods and Services Tax provides a model, both in its structure and in the manner of its implementation, for other contries that are considering sales tax reform'.

An extensive analysis of the incidence of indirect taxes in New Zealand and the likely effects of the introduction of a Goods and Services Tax (GST) was carried out by Scott *et al.* (1985), along with supporting material by Broad and Bacica (1985). Their analysis involved a detailed study using the unit record data from the New Zealand Household Expenditure Survey. These authors measured, for a range of income groups and household types, the impact effects of the changes assuming full shifting of indirect taxes to consumers in the form of price rises. Hence, no attempt was made to allow for behavioural changes such as substitution between commodity groups or changes in labour supply behaviour by household members. The analysis necessarily used a partial equilibrium framework, so no allowance was made for changes in tax-exclusive goods prices or factor prices.

The following analysis adopts all the assumptions of the earlier study, with two exceptions. Consumer responses to price changes are modelled and money measures of welfare changes (compensating and equivalent variations) are calculated for each income group. The conclusions of the earlier study were based on estimated profiles of indirect tax paid in relation to household income. The present study is, however, more limited in that it has not been able to examine different household types (by size, composition and age of head), and unit record data have not been used.

Section 8.1 derives the expressions for compensating and equivalent variations in the case of the linear expenditure system. As these results are described in chapter 5, the discussion is brief. The method used to estimate the required parameters is described in section 8.2. Section 8.3 presents the results relating to the introduction of a Goods and Services Tax (GST) in New Zealand.

8.1   The Welfare Effects of Price Changes

8.1.1   The Linear Expenditure System

The utility function, in multiplicative form, is:

$$U = \prod_i (x_i - \gamma_i)^{\beta_i} \qquad (8.1)$$

with $x_i \geq \gamma_i$, and $0 \leq \beta_i \leq 1$. Furthermore, γ_i is committed expenditure on good i, and $\sum \beta_i = 1$. Maximisation subject to the budget constraint $m = \sum p_i x_i$ gives rise to the linear expenditure functions:

$$p_i x_i = \gamma_i p_i + \beta_i \left(m - \sum_j p_j \gamma_j \right) \tag{8.2}$$

If $A = \sum_i p_i \gamma_i$ and $B = \prod_i (p_i/\beta_i)^{\beta_i}$, the expenditure function is:

$$E(p, U) = A + BU \tag{8.3}$$

8.1.2 Compensating and Equivalent Variations

Suppose that prices change from p_0 to p_1 as a result of the imposition of indirect taxes. The compensating variation is the difference between the minimum expenditure required to achieve the original utility level, at the new price, and the initial total expenditure. Hence:

$$CV = E(p_1, U_0) - E(p_0, U_0)$$

Substituting using (8.3) gives, where subscripts refer to the set of prices used:

$$CV = A_0 \left[\frac{A_1}{A_0} + \frac{B_1}{B_0} \left(\frac{m_0}{A_0} - 1 \right) \right] - m_0 \tag{8.4}$$

The term A_1/A_0 is a Laspeyres type of price index, using the committed consumption of each good as the weight. If $\dot{p}_i$ denotes the proportionate change in the price of the ith good, then $p_{1i} = p_{0i}(1 + \dot{p}_i)$ and:

$$\frac{A_1}{A_0} = 1 + \sum_i s_i \dot{p}_i \tag{8.5}$$

where $s_i = p_{0i}\gamma_i / \sum_i p_{0i}\gamma_i$. The term B_1/B_0 simplifies to $\prod (p_{1i}/p_{0i})^{\beta_i}$, which is a weighted geometric mean of price relatives. Expressing this in terms of the proportionate changes gives:

$$\frac{B_1}{B_0} = \prod_i (1 + \dot{p}_i)^{\beta_i} \tag{8.6}$$

It is therefore possible to use (8.4), with (8.5) and (8.6), to calculate the compensating variation, given a set of proportionate price changes and the coefficients β_i, along with the initial cost of committed expenditure for each good, $p_i \gamma_i$. A feature of the results is that information about separate values of γ_i and p_i are not required.

The equivalent variation is the difference between the post-change total expenditure and the minimum expenditure required to achieve post-change utility at the pre-change prices. Hence:

$$EV = E\left(p_1, U_1\right) - E\left(p_0, U_1\right) \tag{8.7}$$

so that:

$$EV = m_1 - A_0 \left[1 + \frac{B_0}{B_1}\left(\frac{m_1}{A_0} - \frac{A_1}{A_0}\right)\right] \tag{8.8}$$

8.1.3   Comparing Tax Structures

In the following empirical analysis, separate parameters of the LES and therefore welfare changes are estimated for each of a range of different income, or total expenditure, groups. The price changes, $\dot{p}_i$, are regarded as arising from the change in the indirect tax structure. The above results are then used to calculate compensating and equivalent variations for each income group.

An advantage of the equivalent variation is that it can be linked to the concept of equivalent income, m_e, defined in chapter 4. Using pre-change prices as reference prices, it is known that $m_e = m - EV$. The pre-change equivalent income is m and the proportionate change in equivalent income following a set of price changes is thus EV/m. If this ratio is the same for all households, then any relative measure of inequality of equivalent income is unchanged as a result of the tax change. Hence, values of this ratio are reported below along with the absolute values of equivalent variations for each income group. This approach has the desirable property that an equal proportionate increase in all prices gives rise to the same ratio of welfare loss to total expenditure for each household; for example, a proportionate increase of θ in all prices produces a CV/m ratio of θ, and an EV/m ratio of $1/\left(1 + \theta\right)$, for each household.

This argument also shows that it is not appropriate to divide the equivalent variation by disposable income (that is, post-tax-and-transfer income) or even total pre-tax income, rather than total expenditure, when the aim is to examine the welfare changes for each household arising from a set of price changes. Some commentators argue that low-income households face a higher burden of indirect taxes than high-income households simply because the latter save relatively more, though it is often forgotten that savings are ultimately spent. However, in the present context savings are irrelevant. In considering differences in savings patterns among households, the real issue concerns the precise tax treatment of those savings. For example, it would be of interest to examine differential real rates of return obtained by savers in different income groups, but that is a separate question.

8.2   Estimation of the LES

This section describes the method used to estimate the required elasticities and parameter values for the linear expenditure function in each income (total expenditure) group; for further detail, see chapter 5. From equation (8.2), the own-price elasticity of demand for the linear expenditure system is:

$$\eta_{ii} = -\frac{\beta_i}{p_i x_i} \left\{ m - \sum_{j \neq i} p_j \gamma_j \right\} \tag{8.9}$$

This can be rearranged as:

$$\eta_{ii} = \frac{\gamma_i (1 - \beta_i)}{x_i} - 1 \tag{8.10}$$

If $w_i = p_i x_i / m$ is the expenditure share of the ith good, the income (total expenditure) elasticity is:

$$e_i = \frac{\beta_i}{w_i} \tag{8.11}$$

Household budget data give, for each of a range of total expenditure (or income) groups, the expenditure weights, w_i, for each commodity group. The published expenditure weights from the 1993/94 HES for New Zealand are available for nine total expenditure groups. However, the present analysis excludes the category 'net capital outlay and related expenditure' which is too unreliable and contains capital gains.

These weights can be used to find, for each income group, the set of income elasticities, using the result that:

$$e_i = 1 + \frac{\dot{w_i}}{\dot{m_i}} \tag{8.12}$$

where the dots indicate proportionate changes (moving from one income group to the next). However, the raw weights cannot be used directly because they would give rise to numerous negative income elasticities. It is necessary first to obtain a smooth relationship between the weights and total expenditure. This is carried out by estimating, for each commodity group, the following relationship:

$$w_i = a_i + b_i \log(m) \tag{8.13}$$

which generally provides a good fit. Using the estimated values from the fitted regression lines, equation (8.12) was used to calculate the income elasticities. Having calculated the e_is, the corresponding values of β_i can be obtained using the result in (8.11), whereby $\beta_i = e_i w_i$.

Consider the calculation of committed expenditure for each commodity group and income group. If a value of the own-price elasticity of demand is available using extraneous information for each good at each income level, equation (8.10) can be used, after rearrangement, since:

$$p_i \gamma_i = \frac{m w_i (1 + \eta_{ii})}{1 - \beta_i} \tag{8.14}$$

The required set of own-price elasticities may be obtained using the Frisch (1959) result for additive utility functions. In particular, Frisch showed that:

$$\eta_{ii} = e_i \left\{ \frac{1}{\xi} - w_i \left(1 + \frac{e_i}{\xi} \right) \right\} \tag{8.15}$$

The outstanding problem is that in using (8.15) it is required to have values of ξ for each income group. Unfortunately, estimates are not available, so it is necessary to specify a pattern using *a priori* assumptions. A specification for the variation in ξ with m is the following:

$$\log\left(-\xi\right) = 17.5 - 2.2\log\left(m + 450\right) \tag{8.16}$$

This gives values of ξ ranging from -19.73 for the lowest income group to -3.7 for the highest income group. Sensitivity analyses were carried out by investigating the effects of different parameter values for the specification in (8.16), but the comparisons between tax structures shown below were not significantly affected.

8.3 The Introduction of a GST

8.3.1 The Indirect Tax System

Before the GST was introduced, a range of wholesale taxes existed, along with taxes on alcoholic beverages, tobacco products, petroleum fuels and motor vehicles. For present purposes, it is required to express these indirect taxes in terms of *ad valorem* tax-exclusive rates on commodity groups that correspond with those used by the Household Expenditure Survey, since the latter data are used to calculate the required elasticities for a range of income groups. This is not a straightforward exercise, as not all taxes are expressed as *ad valorem* rates and there is not always a direct correspondence between commodity groups.

The wholesale and other indirect tax rates were taken from the Statistics New Zealand computer files used in the Broad and Bacica (1985) study. These rates were used to construct appropriate rates for the Household Expenditure Survey commodities, as shown in Table 8.1.

For use with the framework presented in section 8.1, it is necessary to convert these rates into equivalent percentage price increases, so that it is possible to examine the welfare loss associated with the imposition of these rates (assumed to be fully passed on to consumers). Suppose the tax-exclusive price is p_E, the tax-inclusive price is p_I and the wholesale price is p_W. If q is the wholesale margin, then $p_E = p_W\left(1 + q\right)$ and a wholesale tax rate of t

Table 8.1: Wholesale Tax Rates

HES commodity group	Tax	q^*	q
Property maintenance goods	0.10	0.20	0.25
Home oppliances	0.30	0.25	0.33
Household equipment	0.10	0.25	0.33
Utensils, furniture	0.10	0.20	0.25
Floor coverings	0.10	0.20	0.25
Household textiles	0.10	0.20	0.25
Household supplies	0.10	0.20	0.25
Road vehicles	0.30	0.10	0.11
Vehicle ownership expenses	0.20	0.20	0.25
Tobacco products	0.40	0.20	0.25
Alcohol	0.25	0.20	0.25
Toiletries and cosmetics	0.20	0.20	0.25
Personal goods	0.30	0.20	0.25
Pets, racehorses and livestock	0.20	0.20	0.25
Publications, stationery	0.25	0.20	0.25
Office equip, leisure and rec. goods	0.20	0.20	0.25
Recreational vehicles	0.10	0.20	0.25
Goods n.e.c.	0.10	0.20	0.25

gives rise to a tax-inclusive price given by $p_I = p_E + p_W t$, or:

$$p_I = p_W \left(1 + q + t\right) \qquad (8.17)$$

If the wholesale tax rate increases by the absolute amount $\triangle t$, the proportionate increase in p_I is given by:

$$\dot{p} = \frac{\triangle t}{1 + q + t} \qquad (8.18)$$

Hence if the initial tax rate is zero, the proportionate increase is $\triangle t / \left(1 + q\right)$. Values of retail margins are given in Broad and Bacica (1985, p.56), but because the emphasis of their work is on calculating the tax revenue, they define the margins slightly differently. They give values of q^*, where $p_W = p_E \left(1 - q^*\right)$, which means that $q = \{1 / \left(1 - q^*\right)\} - 1$. These values are also shown in Table 8.1.

Consider next the case of a consumption tax imposed on the tax-exclusive price rather than the wholesale price. If t denotes the tax rate, then $p_I = p_E (1 + t)$, and if this rate increases by the Δt, the proportionate increase in the price is now given by:

$$\dot{p} = \frac{\Delta t}{1 + t} \qquad (8.19)$$

Comparison of (8.18) and (8.19) shows, as expected, that a given tax rate change imposes a smaller price change for a wholesale tax compared with a sales tax, reflecting the different tax bases. The introduction of a sales tax from a base of a zero rate thus implies that the proportionate price change is equal to the tax rate, given by Δt.

Consider next the effect of a transition from a wholesale tax to a consumption tax, involving a change in both the tax rate and the tax base. Substituting for $p_E = (1 + q) p_W$, the new price, following conversion to a GST and a change in the tax rate of Δt, is given by $p_W (1 + q) (1 + t + \Delta t)$, so that the proportionate change, measured from the price given in equation (8.17), is given by:

$$\dot{p} = \frac{(1 + q) (1 + t + \Delta t)}{1 + q + t} - 1 \qquad (8.20)$$

which can be simplified to give:

$$\dot{p} = \frac{tq + (1 + q) \Delta t}{1 + q + t} \qquad (8.21)$$

Hence the percentage price change resulting exclusively from a change in the tax base, where $\Delta t = 0$, is given by $tq / (1 + q + t)$.

In several cases, such as alcohol, tobacco and motor vehicles, the pre-GST taxes were left in place and GST was added. If t represents the pre-GST rate expressed as a wholesale tax and if t^* now represents the tax-exclusive GST rate, the tax-inclusive price is $p_W (1 + q + t) (1 + t^*)$. Hence the proportionate price increase, $(p_I - p_E) / p_E$, can be shown to be:

$$\dot{p} = t^* + \frac{t (1 + t^*)}{1 + q} \qquad (8.22)$$

This is the price change used when examining the post-GST structure. When examining the once-and-for-all change in these cases, it can be shown that the

Table 8.2: Pre-GST Indirect Taxes

No.	m	CV	CV/m	EV	EV/m
1	284.40	15.34	0.0539	14.59	0.0513
2	332.20	17.95	0.0540	17.07	0.0514
3	387.80	21.02	0.0542	19.99	0.0515
4	505.60	27.39	0.0542	26.07	0.0516
5	566.20	30.57	0.0540	29.10	0.0514
6	624.90	33.71	0.0539	32.11	0.0514
7	766.60	40.93	0.0534	39.03	0.0509
8	876.80	46.55	0.0531	44.42	0.0507
9	1121.70	58.33	0.0520	55.77	0.0497

appropriate proportionate change for these groups is the same as in equation
(8.19).

8.3.2 Empirical Estimates

The pre-GST indirect tax system can be regarded as imposing a set of price
increases, compared with a situation of no taxes, given by equation (8.18)
with $t = 0$ and Δt equal to the rate as specified in Table 8.1, with all other
values of $\dot{p}$ set equal to zero. The welfare changes for each income group are
given in Table 8.2, expressed in dollars per week. The values of m given in the
first column correspond to the average weekly total expenditure of households
in the specified income group. These total expenditures are assumed to
remain fixed when the tax system is changed; only the allocation between
commodity groups changes. The nine groups correspond to the groups in the
1993/94 Household Expenditure Survey. The compensating and equivalent
variations are given, along with their values expressed as proportions of total
expenditure.

It can be seen from Table 8.2 that, except for the slight reductions in
the highest three groups, there is very little variation in these ratios. It
could, therefore, be argued that the pre-GST system of indirect taxes did
not impose a systematically higher burden on lower-income households.

Following the introduction of the GST in New Zealand, the rates imposed on road vehicles, vehicle ownership expenses, tobacco products and

alcohol were held constant. However, a uniform tax-exclusive rate of 0.10 was imposed on all goods and services, with the exception of residential rents, which have a zero rate. Presumably this zero rating of rents was because the implicit rental from owner-occupied housing remains untaxed. The New Zealand GST therefore has a very broad tax base compared with those of many countries which have a range of exemptions and zero rating or which use lower rates (for example, in the case of food and also domestic fuel and power).

Two approaches to the analysis of the GST were carried out. First, as in the pre-GST calculations, a comparison was made of no taxes compared with the GST; results are given in Table 8.3. Secondly, the effects of the once-and-for-all transition were examined by using equation (8.19), with the values of t set at their pre-GST levels and the values of Δt calculated accordingly. In this case, it is necessary to allow the different tax base used where wholesale taxes are relevant. The results are given in Table 8.4.

Finally, the welfare effects of a modified GST structure are reported in Table 8.5, where exemptions are given for food (except meals outside the home) and domestic fuel and power. These groups are exempt in many countries, or have lower rates than the standard rate. These exemptions have been examined using the standard GST rate of 0.10, which means that total revenue is lower. A revenue neutral comparison would involve a slightly higher rate, and consequently very slightly more progression than is shown in Table 8.5. However, these results support the point, often made in this context, that exemptions are an expensive method of purchasing a small amount of progression.

It should be stressed that when the Goods and Services Tax was introduced in New Zealand, comprehensive adjustments to transfer payments were also made.

8.4 Conclusions

This chapter has examined compensating and equivalent variations, for a range of income groups, resulting from indirect tax reform and inflation in

Table 8.3: Post-GST Indirect Taxes

No.	m	CV	CV/m	EV	EV/m
1	284.40	31.86	0.1120	28.65	0.1007
2	332.20	37.40	0.1126	33.58	0.1011
3	387.80	43.94	0.1133	39.45	0.1017
4	505.60	57.57	0.1139	51.77	0.1024
5	566.20	64.40	0.1137	57.94	0.1023
6	624.90	71.18	0.1139	64.06	0.1025
7	766.60	86.82	0.1133	78.29	0.1021
8	876.80	99.19	0.1131	89.48	0.1020
9	1121.70	125.41	0.1118	113.53	0.1012

Table 8.4: Once-and-for-all Changes from GST

No.	m	CV	CV/m	EV	EV/m
1	284.40	14.46	0.0508	13.75	0.0483
2	332.20	17.05	0.0513	16.20	0.0488
3	387.80	20.13	0.0519	19.11	0.0493
4	505.60	26.59	0.0526	25.25	0.0499
5	566.20	29.87	0.0527	28.36	0.0501
6	624.90	33.11	0.0530	31.44	0.0503
7	766.60	40.70	0.0531	38.65	0.0504
8	876.80	46.77	0.0533	44.39	0.0506
9	1121.70	59.96	0.0535	56.93	0.0507

Table 8.5: A Modified GST

No.	m	CV	CV/m	EV	EV/m
1	284.40	25.17	0.0885	22.99	0.0808
2	332.20	29.98	0.0902	27.29	0.0822
3	387.80	35.75	0.0922	32.51	0.0838
4	505.60	47.95	0.0948	43.55	0.0861
5	566.20	54.19	0.0957	49.20	0.0869
6	624.90	60.41	0.0967	54.84	0.0878
7	766.60	74.96	0.0978	68.06	0.0888
8	876.80	86.45	0.0986	78.54	0.0896
9	1121.70	111.13	0.0991	101.03	0.0901

New Zealand. The method involved the use of the linear expenditure system, estimated for each of a range of income (or total expenditure) groups.

The results confirm those of previous studies which found that previous indirect taxes in New Zealand (the various wholesale sales taxes, along with others such as those on alcohol, tobacco and petroleum fuels) did not have a substantially larger impact on low-income groups than on high-income groups. Furthermore, the abolition of the wholesale tax system and the introduction of the goods and services tax does not appear to impose higher welfare losses, expressed as ratios of total expenditure, on those groups with relatively low expenditure. The New Zealand general consumption tax has the advantage of a very broad tax base, compared with many countries which have a range of exemptions and goods that are zero-rated. However, it was found that the degree of progressivity that would be introduced into the system by the use of exemptions on food and domestic fuel and power is very low.

In the calculation of the welfare effects of price changes, those changes have so far (in the present chapter and in chapter 7) arisen from reforms to the indirect tax system. However, relative prices also change from year to year as part of the process of inflation. The distributional effects of inflationary price changes are examined in the following chapter.

Chapter 9

The Distributional Effects of Inflation

Distributional implications of inflation exist because of the fact that prices do not all change by the same proportion over time. If there is a systematic tendency for the price of those goods which form a relatively higher proportion of the total expenditure of low-income households to increase relatively more than other goods, inflation produces adverse effects on the distribution of real income. The effect of differential price changes on welfare also depends on the extent to which households substitute away from those goods whose prices increase relatively more. Studies of inflation in other countries, using a variety of approaches, have found a small effect of this type; see Muellbauer (1974) for the UK, and Blinder and Esaki (1978), Stoker (1986), Slottje (1987) and Slesnick (1990) for the US.

This chapter examines the redistributive effect of price changes in Australia over the 16 year period from 1980 to 1995, and the effects of inflation in New Zealand over the period 1993 to 1995. The distributional effects of inflation are examined in two ways. First, it examines the way in which equivalent variations vary with household income. Secondly, values of several alternative measures of inequality are reported, for a range of degrees of aversion towards inequality. The inequality measures are based on the distribution of equivalent income, defined in chapter 4. It should be borne in mind that the analysis is based entirely on consumption and therefore ignores wealth accumulation and changes in asset prices.

The estimates of the distributional effects are based on the use of the linear expenditure system, LES, which is applied to each income group separately. This follows the approach set out in chapter 5. Muellbauer (1974) measured welfare changes using estimates of the linear expenditure system based on aggregate data; but even if only a single set of parameters is used, the ratio of the compensating and equivalent variations to total household expenditure is higher in lower-income groups if the price of 'necessities' increases by relatively more than that of 'luxuries'.

The cost of the present approach is that it involves a large increase in the number of parameters to be estimated, so that very strong restrictions are imposed. Estimation of the LES for each income group is based on the expressions obtained by Frisch (1959) for the elasticities of demand for additive utility functions, of which the LES is a special case. The empirical results reported here use the 16 commodity groups for which data are given in the Australian Household Expenditure Survey. In the New Zealand Household Expenditure Survey, 60 commodity groups are used.

Section 9.1 presents the expressions for compensating and equivalent variations in the case of the linear expenditure system. These are given in more detail in chapter 5. The effects of inflation in Australia are then examined in section 9.2. The approach involves the application of proportionate annual price changes, for each year in turn, to the LES utility function parameters estimated using data for 1989. Section 9.2 therefore considers the following question: what would be the effect on the welfare of 1989 households of applying alternative sets of proportionate price changes? The effects of inflation in New Zealand are examined in section 9.3.

9.1 Welfare Effects of Price Changes

This section briefly derives the expressions used to calculate the welfare effects of price changes using the linear expenditure system: further details are given in chapter 5.

9.1.1 The Linear Expenditure System

The direct utility function, in multiplicative form, is:

$$U = \prod_i (x_i - \gamma_i)^{\beta_i} \tag{9.1}$$

where $x_i \geq \gamma_i$ denotes the consumption of good i; $0 \leq \beta_i \leq 1$; γ_i is the committed consumption of good i; and $\sum \beta_i = 1$. Define the terms A and B respectively as $\sum_i p_i \gamma_i$ and $\prod (p_i/\beta_i)^{\beta_i}$. The expenditure function, $E(p, U)$, is:

$$E(p, U) = A + BU \tag{9.2}$$

9.1.2 Equivalent Variations

Suppose that the vector of prices changes from p_0 to p_1. The equivalent variation, EV, is the difference between the post-change total expenditure and the minimum expenditure required to achieve post-change utility at the pre-change prices, so that $EV = E(p_1, U_1) - E(p_0, U_1)$. Substituting for E using (9.2) gives:

$$EV = m_1 - A_0 \left[1 + \frac{B_0}{B_1} \left(\frac{m_1}{A_0} - \frac{A_1}{A_0} \right) \right] \tag{9.3}$$

The term A_1/A_0 is a Laspeyres type of price index, using the committed consumption of each good as the weight. The term B_1/B_0 simplifies to $\prod (p_{1i}/p_{0i})^{\beta_i}$, which is a weighted geometric mean of price relatives. It is possible to calculate the compensating and equivalent variations, given m_0, m_1, the set of proportionate price changes and the coefficients β_i, along with the initial cost of committed expenditure for each good, $p_i \gamma_i$.

9.1.3 Equivalent Incomes

Equivalent income is the value of income, m_e, which, at some reference set of prices, p_r, gives the same utility as the actual income level; see chapter 4. As is usual in this type of static framework, income and total expenditure are treated as synonymous. In terms of the indirect utility function, m_e is therefore defined $V(p_r, m_e) = V(p, m)$, and using the expenditure function gives $m_e = E(p_r, V(p, m))$. For the linear expenditure system:

$$m_e = \sum_i p_{ri}\gamma_i + \left\{\prod_i \left(\frac{p_{ri}}{p_i}\right)^{\beta_i}\right\}\left\{m - \sum_j p_j\gamma_j\right\} \qquad (9.4)$$

The effect on welfare of a change in prices and income can then be measured in terms of a change in equivalent incomes, from m_{0e} to m_{1e}, where, as before, the indices 0 and 1 refer to pre- and post-change values respectively. Furthermore, values of a social welfare function can be calculated using the distribution of values of m_{0e} and m_{1e} so that, according to the value judgements implicit in the welfare function, a change can be judged in terms of its overall effect.

A feature of equivalent income is that it ensures that alternative situations are evaluated using a common set of reference prices. Consider the use of pre-change prices as reference prices, so that $p_{ri} = p_{0i}$ for all i. In this case it can be shown that the post-change equivalent income is the value of actual income after the change less the value of the equivalent variation; that is, $m_{1e} = m_1 - EV$.

9.2 Australian Price Changes

The annual percentage price changes for each of the 16 Household Expenditure Survey (HES) commodity groups over the period 1980 to 1995 are shown in Tables 9.1 and 9.2. The price index data for each subgroup were obtained from March publications of the Consumer Price Index (ABS 6401.0). A problem arises because the commodity groups used by the HES do not correspond to those used in compiling the consumer price index (CPI) data. In some cases an approximation only could be used; for example, 'personal care products' was used for 'toiletries and cosmetics'. In obtaining the price changes for each group, the subgroups were combined using weights given by the 'contribution to total CPI' data. The HES commodity group 'household capital goods' has no adequate CPI equivalent, so price data for this group were obtained from March publications of the House Building Materials Price

Table 9.1: Australian Price Changes

	H'ng Costs	Power	Food	Alcohol	Tobacco	Clothing	Equip
1980	7.60	15.20	15.00	5.60	6.00	6.70	6.35
1981	10.10	14.30	9.70	8.00	4.60	7.60	10.02
1982	11.10	15.70	7.70	9.70	8.70	7.00	8.12
1983	10.60	21.10	9.00	12.30	18.50	6.10	8.69
1984	6.80	7.10	8.70	9.00	22.00	6.10	6.88
1985	7.20	6.50	4.40	7.10	7.70	6.20	3.25
1986	9.00	5.80	8.30	8.30	13.60	8.30	10.20
1987	7.20	4.40	7.90	10.20	11.40	10.10	7.31
1988	6.60	5.90	4.60	7.80	8.00	7.10	7.55
1989	11.60	4.50	9.40	3.20	10.30	7.30	5.87
1990	17.00	4.30	6.20	7.50	12.40	5.20	6.04
1991	1.60	5.60	5.20	7.10	12.40	4.90	4.45
1992	-4.80	4.30	1.30	3.20	8.90	1.30	1.02
1993	-3.80	5.40	2.70	2.70	23.60	1.10	0.03
1994	-0.70	1.10	0.70	3.10	12.70	-1.10	2.94
1995	9.70	0.80	3.10	3.60	7.10	-0.10	1.37

Index (ABS, Cat. no. 6408.0).

The higher inflation during the early and late 1980s, along with the generally lower inflation during the 1990s, is clearly shown in the table. The price changes show a wide dispersion across commodity groups. The changes in the CPI for the corresponding years are given by: 10.5, 9.4, 10.5, 11.5, 5.9, 4.4, 9.2, 9.4, 6.9, 6.8, 8.6, 4.9, 1.7, 1.2, 1.4, and 3.9.

The LES parameters for each of a range of total expenditure or income groups were obtained using the Household Expenditure Survey for 1989. The approach involved the application of proportionate annual price changes, for each year in turn, to the LES utility function parameters estimated using data for 1989. The results therefore consider the following question: what would be the effect on the welfare of 1989 households of applying alternative sets of proportionate price changes?

The first stage involves producing a matrix of budget shares. The average budget shares were calculated for each commodity group within 29 total expenditure groups (giving 29 separate sets of LES parameter estimates from

Table 9.2: Australian Price Changes

	Service	Hlth Care	Trans	E'tain	Pers Care	Mort	Cap Gds
1980	8.39	27.80	11.60	10.18	8.80	0.00	15.30
1981	12.79	2.10	10.90	8.21	14.45	0.00	10.30
1982	11.22	46.10	9.80	11.28	9.23	0.00	10.00
1983	11.92	22.50	13.60	9.55	15.55	0.00	6.70
1984	5.81	-25.30	7.20	4.84	6.90	0.00	7.70
1985	4.99	-21.90	5.80	2.82	7.12	0.00	8.20
1986	9.05	7.90	10.90	9.80	8.94	0.00	6.30
1987	5.59	26.90	11.20	9.25	11.38	0.00	6.80
1988	5.89	14.90	6.70	7.62	6.53	3.70	8.40
1989	5.85	11.80	2.70	4.24	4.24	15.70	10.90
1990	2.09	6.50	9.90	6.27	5.95	29.70	6.70
1991	3.74	13.10	4.50	4.34	6.35	-2.90	4.10
1992	3.34	20.10	2.90	0.44	2.96	-14.20	-0.60
1993	1.53	-2.40	1.80	2.25	2.11	-11.20	2.90
1994	2.18	4.70	1.70	1.60	3.05	-6.60	4.60
1995	1.10	5.80	3.60	2.86	2.53	22.80	3.10

464 budget shares). The precise method of computing the parameter values and the resulting elasticities is discussed in more detail in chapter 5. This requires a specified variation in the Frisch parameter. Based on these studies and Frisch's own conjectures, the following flexible specification has been found to be useful for the variation in ξ with m:

$$\log\left(-\xi\right) = a - \alpha \log\left(m + \theta\right) \tag{9.5}$$

Suitable parameter values were obtained by experimenting with a range of alternatives. As a starting point, values of ξ corresponding to various values of m, conforming with *a priori* beliefs based on the studies mentioned above, were used to estimate the parameters of (9.5) using an iterative method based on maximum likelihood. The following set of parameters was used for a, α and θ: 15.2, 1.227, 8595.44.

9.2.1 Equivalent Variations

Values of equivalent variations, expressed as ratios of total expenditure, are given in Tables 9.3 and 9.4 for each year and total expenditure group. The arithmetic mean weekly expenditure in each group, measured in cents, is given in the first column of each table. The equivalent variations were evaluated at the mean total expenditure levels by applying the LES parameters appropriate to each group. If the percentage price changes were the same for each commodity group, the equivalent variations (expressed as ratios of total expenditure) would be the same for each total expenditure group. An initial idea of the distributional effect of the price changes can therefore be seen by reading down the columns for each year's price changes.

In the early 1980s the price changes suggest a small systematic higher burden faced by lower income groups. But by the middle to late 1980s this effect becomes negligible, and in some cases the burden faced by the middle income groups is slightly higher than for the lower income groups. There is some suggestion that the periods during which the relative burden borne by the lower income groups is higher coincide with the periods of higher increases in the CPI. Corresponding results for households with and without dependants were reported by Creedy and van de Ven (1997).

9.2.2 Inequality Measures

Any assessment of the redistributive impact of a change cannot escape the use of value judgements. For this reason it is useful to make such judgements explicit by computing a range of inequality measures, reflecting different degrees of aversion towards inequality. Hence, a second analysis was carried out where each set of price changes was applied in turn to each of the 7191 households in the HES. The resulting distribution of equivalent incomes was then obtained and inequality measures were based on that distribution. In calculating the equivalent income for each household, each household was assigned the LES parameter values and elasticities corresponding to the income group in which it fell.

The inequality measures calculated include Atkinson's (1970) measure,

Table 9.3: Ratio of EV to Total Expenditure: All Households 1980-7

	1980	1981	1982	1983	1984	1985	1986	1987
8000.00	0.107	0.090	0.103	0.106	0.058	0.040	0.081	0.081
11581.18	0.106	0.090	0.103	0.105	0.058	0.040	0.081	0.081
14417.82	0.106	0.089	0.103	0.105	0.057	0.039	0.081	0.082
17132.45	0.106	0.089	0.103	0.104	0.057	0.039	0.081	0.083
19732.05	0.105	0.088	0.103	0.104	0.056	0.039	0.081	0.083
22178.05	0.105	0.088	0.103	0.104	0.055	0.038	0.082	0.084
24684.80	0.104	0.088	0.103	0.104	0.055	0.038	0.082	0.084
27227.80	0.104	0.087	0.103	0.103	0.055	0.038	0.082	0.084
29749.50	0.104	0.087	0.103	0.103	0.054	0.038	0.082	0.084
32461.45	0.103	0.087	0.103	0.103	0.054	0.038	0.082	0.085
35035.60	0.103	0.087	0.103	0.103	0.054	0.038	0.082	0.085
37624.65	0.103	0.086	0.102	0.102	0.054	0.038	0.082	0.085
40547.80	0.102	0.086	0.102	0.102	0.054	0.038	0.082	0.085
43534.55	0.102	0.086	0.102	0.102	0.054	0.038	0.082	0.085
46464.40	0.102	0.086	0.101	0.101	0.054	0.038	0.082	0.085
49313.00	0.101	0.086	0.101	0.101	0.054	0.038	0.082	0.085
52223.65	0.101	0.086	0.101	0.101	0.054	0.039	0.082	0.085
55318.80	0.101	0.086	0.101	0.101	0.054	0.039	0.082	0.085
58561.85	0.101	0.086	0.101	0.100	0.054	0.039	0.082	0.085
61798.95	0.100	0.086	0.100	0.100	0.054	0.039	0.082	0.085
65172.60	0.100	0.086	0.100	0.100	0.054	0.039	0.082	0.085
68908.10	0.098	0.086	0.100	0.100	0.054	0.040	0.082	0.085
73162.50	0.099	0.086	0.099	0.099	0.054	0.040	0.082	0.085
78105.30	0.099	0.086	0.099	0.099	0.054	0.040	0.082	0.084
83574.05	0.099	0.086	0.099	0.099	0.054	0.040	0.082	0.084
89947.85	0.099	0.086	0.098	0.098	0.055	0.041	0.082	0.084
97849.60	0.099	0.086	0.097	0.098	0.055	0.042	0.082	0.084
109671.60	0.099	0.086	0.097	0.097	0.056	0.043	0.082	0.084
128647.82	0.100	0.087	0.096	0.095	0.057	0.044	0.081	0.083

Table 9.4: Ratio of EV to Total Expenditure: All Households 1988-95

	1988	1989	1990	1991	1992	1993	1994	1995
8000.00	0.060	0.074	0.075	0.047	0.017	0.016	0.013	0.039
11581.18	0.061	0.073	0.076	0.047	0.017	0.016	0.014	0.039
14417.82	0.061	0.073	0.076	0.047	0.017	0.015	0.014	0.039
17132.45	0.061	0.072	0.077	0.047	0.017	0.015	0.014	0.040
19732.05	0.062	0.072	0.077	0.047	0.017	0.014	0.014	0.040
22178.05	0.062	0.072	0.077	0.046	0.017	0.014	0.014	0.040
24684.80	0.062	0.071	0.078	0.046	0.017	0.014	0.014	0.040
27227.80	0.062	0.071	0.078	0.046	0.016	0.013	0.014	0.040
29749.50	0.063	0.071	0.078	0.046	0.016	0.013	0.014	0.041
32461.45	0.063	0.071	0.079	0.046	0.016	0.013	0.014	0.041
35035.60	0.063	0.070	0.079	0.046	0.016	0.013	0.014	0.041
37624.65	0.063	0.070	0.079	0.046	0.016	0.012	0.014	0.041
40547.80	0.063	0.070	0.079	0.046	0.016	0.012	0.014	0.041
43534.55	0.063	0.070	0.079	0.046	0.015	0.012	0.014	0.044
46464.40	0.064	0.069	0.079	0.046	0.015	0.012	0.014	0.041
49313.00	0.064	0.069	0.080	0.046	0.015	0.012	0.014	0.041
52223.65	0.064	0.069	0.080	0.045	0.015	0.012	0.014	0.040
55318.80	0.064	0.069	0.080	0.045	0.015	0.011	0.014	0.040
58561.85	0.064	0.069	0.080	0.045	0.014	0.011	0.014	0.040
61798.95	0.064	0.068	0.080	0.045	0.014	0.011	0.014	0.040
65172.60	0.064	0.068	0.080	0.045	0.014	0.011	0.014	0.040
68908.10	0.064	0.068	0.080	0.045	0.014	0.011	0.014	0.040
73162.50	0.064	0.068	0.080	0.045	0.013	0.011	0.014	0.040
78105.30	0.064	0.067	0.080	0.045	0.013	0.011	0.014	0.040
83574.05	0.064	0.067	0.080	0.045	0.013	0.011	0.014	0.040
89947.85	0.065	0.067	0.079	0.044	0.013	0.011	0.015	0.039
97849.60	0.065	0.067	0.079	0.044	0.013	0.012	0.015	0.039
109671.60	0.065	0.067	0.078	0.044	0.012	0.012	0.016	0.038
128647.82	0.066	0.068	0.077	0.044	0.011	0.013	0.017	0.037

Table 9.5: Inequality Measures of Equivalent Income: All Households

Year	$A(0.2)$	$A(0.8)$	$A(1.4)$	G	$G(1.2)$	$G(1.6)$	$G(2.4)$
1980	0.0399	0.1582	0.2760	0.3474	0.1124	0.2560	0.4121
1981	0.0397	0.1577	0.2752	0.3468	0.1122	0.2556	0.4114
1982	0.0400	0.1584	0.2761	0.3479	0.1127	0.2565	0.4124
1983	0.0401	0.1587	0.2766	0.3482	0.1129	0.2568	0.4127
1984	0.0396	0.1574	0.2749	0.3464	0.1120	0.2552	0.4109
1985	0.0394	0.1567	0.2738	0.3456	0.1117	0.2545	0.4100
1986	0.0397	0.1574	0.2744	0.3466	0.1123	0.2556	0.4111
1987	0.0397	0.1573	0.2742	0.3467	0.1123	0.2556	0.4110
1988	0.0395	0.1567	0.2735	0.3459	0.1119	0.2549	0.4103
1989	0.0398	0.1581	0.2758	0.3473	0.1124	0.2560	0.4119
1990	0.0397	0.1572	0.2741	0.3465	0.1123	0.2555	0.4109
1991	0.0398	0.1577	0.2751	0.3470	0.1124	0.2558	0.4115
1992	0.0399	0.1581	0.2756	0.3475	0.1126	0.2562	0.4120
1993	0.0397	0.1576	0.2752	0.3468	0.1122	0.2555	0.4113
1994	0.0395	0.1569	0.2739	0.3460	0.1119	0.2549	0.4105
1995	0.0398	0.1577	0.2748	0.3470	0.1125	0.2559	0.4114
Base	0.0397	0.1573	0.2745	0.3465	0.1122	0.2554	0.4110

$A(\varepsilon)$, for various values of the inequality aversion parameter, ε, and the extended Gini measure, $G(v)$, following Yitzhaki (1983), where the parameter v has a similar role to that of ε. When $v = 2$, the value of $G(v)$ corresponds to the standard Gini inequality measure; for further discussion of these measures see, for example, Lambert (1993a, b) and Creedy (1996).

The inequality measures are shown in Table 9.5. The measures for each year can be compared with the 'base' value, which is the inequality of equivalent income with zero proportional price changes in each commodity group. The highest inequality measure, for all degrees of aversion, is for 1983 price changes. This is the year which experienced the largest increase in the CPI over the period investigated. The next highest inequality value is consistently for 1982, irrespective of the measure used; this is also one of the years for which inflation is highest.

For lower degrees of aversion towards inequality, there are several sets of annual price changes for which the inequality of equivalent incomes is less than or equal to that of the 'base' value. For all degrees of aversion, the price changes for 1985, 1988 and 1994 produce reductions relative to the base value. Hence the price changes in those years can be said to impose a higher burden on the higher income groups.

9.3 Inflation in New Zealand

This section examines welfare measures in each income group resulting from imposing the percentage price changes for each commodity group experienced over the period 1993-4 and 1994-5. During these periods the consumer price index (CPI) increased by annual rates of 0.026 and 0.031 for the two periods respectively, but this involved a wide distribution of changes over commodity groups.

Information is available on price indices for 320 commodity groups, along with the weights used in the CPI, for December 1993, 1994 and 1995. These are available in unpublished data on the INFOS Consumer Price Index – All Sections, produced by Statistics New Zealand. The first task is to convert these 320 indices into price changes relating to the classifications used in the Household Expenditure Survey. Where there was no information corresponding to the Household Expenditure Survey category, the CPI change over the period was assigned to the Household Expenditure Survey group. The resulting proportionate changes are given in Table 9.6. This shows that even over a single year, there is a wide dispersion in the price increases over commodity groups.

The equivalent variations resulting from these changes are given in Table 9.7, for 1993-4 and 1994-5. The changes for the earlier period do not show any systematic variation with income, but for the later period it can be seen that there is an increase in the equivalent variation, expressed as a ratio of total expenditure, as the latter increases. However, the differences are small.

9.4 Conclusions

This chapter has examined the distributional effects of the differential price changes associated with inflation in Australia over the period 1980 to 1995,

Table 9.6: New Zealand Price Changes

No.	1993-4	No.	1993-4	No.	1994-5	No.	1994-5
1	0.026	31	0.009	1	0.031	31	-0.028
2	0.025	32	0.022	2	0.047	32	-0.026
3	-0.049	33	0.007	3	-0.058	33	-0.027
4	-0.019	34	0.026	4	-0.010	34	0.031
5	-0.031	35	0.026	5	-0.018	35	0.031
6	-0.009	36	0.011	6	0.013	36	0.080
7	0.001	37	0.052	7	0.027	37	-0.024
8	0.134	38	0.017	8	-0.012	38	0.022
9	-0.018	39	-0.004	9	-0.019	39	-0.032
10	0.001	40	0.026	10	0.017	40	0.031
11	0.120	41	0.003	11	0.085	41	0.032
12	0.110	42	0.021	12	0.184	42	0.038
13	0.026	43	0.029	13	0.031	43	0.066
14	0.011	44	-0.010	14	0.021	44	0.018
15	0.011	45	0.004	15	0.021	45	0.013
16	0.006	46	0.026	16	0.012	46	0.031
17	0.046	47	0.015	17	0.054	47	0.065
18	-0.009	48	0.011	18	-0.037	48	0.014
19	-0.009	49	0.035	19	-0.037	49	0.028
20	0.030	50	0.026	20	0.023	50	0.031
21	0.026	51	0.026	21	0.031	51	0.031
22	0.057	52	0.026	22	0.006	52	0.031
23	0.005	53	0.088	23	-0.034	53	0.054
24	-0.024	54	0.026	24	-0.005	54	0.031
25	0.026	55	-0.011	25	0.031	55	0.073
26	-0.001	56	0.026	26	-0.015	56	0.031
27	-0.013	57	0.026	27	-0.008	57	0.031
28	-0.027	58	0.026	28	-0.014	58	0.031
29	-0.042	59	0.026	29	-0.043	59	0.031
30	-0.017	60	0.026	30	0.041	60	0.031

Table 9.7: New Zealand Price Changes 1993-5

No.	m	EV	EV/m	EV	EV/m
		1993-4		1994-5	
1	284.40	8.28	0.0291	8.38	0.0295
2	332.20	9.56	0.0288	9.95	0.0299
3	387.80	10.97	0.0283	11.78	0.0304
4	505.60	14.06	0.0278	15.78	0.0312
5	566.20	15.76	0.0278	17.94	0.0317
6	624.90	17.30	0.0277	20.00	0.0320
7	766.60	21.40	0.0279	25.23	0.0329
8	876.80	24.42	0.0279	29.29	0.0334
9	1121.70	31.83	0.0284	38.79	0.0346

using equivalent variations and equivalent incomes, and in New Zealand over the period 1993-1995. The linear expenditure system was applied to a range of income groups rather than using a single set of parameters. The analysis was applied to all households in the Household Expenditure Survey. The price changes were found to impose a relatively higher burden on lower income groups in some years, although in other years the higher income groups were relatively more affected. The years when the inequality of equivalent incomes was highest coincide with years of high overall inflation.

However, the measured effects on inequality are low: the highest increase in inequality over the 'base' value as a result of differential price changes is less than 1 per cent. Hence, over the period investigated, inflation does not appear to have had substantial redistributive effects, and in some cases a small progressive effect was observed. In considering these results, it should be remembered that the analysis was restricted to household consumption, and did not consider the distributional implications of capital gains resulting from changes in asset prices, particularly housing prices, over the period.

Chapter 10

Welfare Costs of Monopoly

The aim of this chapter is to examine the distributional effects of monopoly. When discussing low estimates of the aggregate welfare loss from monopoly, Stigler (1966, p.34) remarked that 'economists might serve a more useful purpose if they fought fires or termites instead of monopoly'. However, it is quite possible that small aggregate welfare losses can coexist with large distributional effects. For example, after examining a hypothetical model which allowed both the aggregative and distributional effects of monopoly to be computed, McKenzie (1983, p.173) suggested that 'Stigler's conclusion may have been reached too hastily' and 'economists should have looked more closely at the income distributional effects of monopoly'.

There seem to have been very few studies of the distributional effects of monopoly, which is regarded more broadly as the absence of competition rather than the existence of a single seller. Creedy and Dixon (1998) estimated relative values of consumers' surplus measures for a range of income, or total expenditure, groups in Australia, using a model in which price elasticities differ between income groups. The present chapter extends that analysis in several ways. First, equivalent variations are calculated instead of using the consumers' surplus approximation. Secondly, inequality measures are based on the complete distribution of equivalent incomes, using all households in the Household Expenditure Survey. This allows for a range of inequality aversion coefficients to be investigated. Thirdly, departures from the simple profit maximisation model are used. Finally, the more recent

165

Household Expenditure Survey for 1993 is used. It should be stressed that the partial equilibrium approach inevitably relies on the use of very strong assumptions, so the results need to be treated with caution.

The analysis is based on a comparison of the actual prices with those that would otherwise be found if all goods were produced under competitive conditions. It requires two basic ingredients. First, it is necessary to have a way of measuring the welfare and distributional effects of a set of proportional price changes. The welfare measures and responses of consumers to price changes are based on the use of the linear expenditure system, as described in chapter 5, and estimated separately for each of a range of income groups. Section 10.1 describes the way in which the welfare measures are calculated for each household.

Secondly, it is necessary to specify the counterfactual. In the present context the price changes are the price differences from a comparison of monopoly pricing with prices that would otherwise arise in a competitive market. Section 10.2 discusses alternative models of monopoly pricing. The term monopoly is interpreted here as the absence of competition, rather than the existence of a single seller in each market.

Section 10.3 presents the empirical results. If the prices of all commodities were to increase by the same proportion (in the hypothetical movement from competition to monopolistic markets), then there would be no distributional effects. The percentage change in the equivalent income of each household would be the same irrespective of its expenditure pattern. However, if the goods which form a larger share of the expenditure of lower-income households typically increase in price by relatively more than other goods, then a measure of inequality would be expected to increase. Such an increase is found in section 10.3. Comparisons with the use of the consumers' surplus measure, following the method of Creedy and Dixon (1998), are reported in section 10.5.

10.1 The Welfare Effects of Price Changes

This section shows how welfare effects can be obtained using the linear expenditure system. Following chapter 5, the welfare measures are based on estimates of the LES for each of a range of total expenditure groups. Households within each group are assumed to have the same preferences, but these preferences are allowed to vary with total expenditure. The strong *a priori* restrictions underlying this approach represent the cost of obtaining welfare measures with limited data.

10.1.1 The Linear Expenditure System

The direct utility function underlying the linear expenditure system, in multiplicative form, is:

$$U = \prod_i (x_i - \gamma_i)^{\beta_i} \tag{10.1}$$

with $x_i \geq \gamma_i$, $0 \leq \beta_i \leq 1$, γ_i is committed expenditure on good i, and $\sum \beta_i = 1$. If $A = \sum_i p_i \gamma_i$ and $B = \prod (p_i/\beta_i)^{\beta_i}$, the expenditure function is given by:

$$E(p, U) = A + BU \tag{10.2}$$

The LES is applied to each income group separately, so that income (or total expenditure) subscripts (suppressed here for convenience) can be added to the coefficients γ and β.

10.1.2 Equivalent Variations

Suppose that prices change from p_0 to p_1. The level of total expenditure remains unchanged at m (in view of the partial equilibrium nature of the analysis). The equivalent variation is the difference between the post-change total expenditure and the minimum expenditure required to achieve post-change utility at the pre-change prices. Hence:

$$EV = E(p_1, U_1) - E(p_0, U_1) \tag{10.3}$$

Substituting (10.2) into (10.3) gives, where subscripts refer to the set of prices used:

$$EV = m - A_0 \left[1 + \frac{B_0}{B_1} \left(\frac{m}{A_0} - \frac{A_1}{A_0} \right) \right] \tag{10.4}$$

The term A_1/A_0 is a Laspeyres type of price index, using the committed consumption of each good as the weight. If $\dot{p}_i$ denotes the proportionate change in the price of the ith good, then $p_{1i} = p_{0i}(1 + \dot{p}_i)$ and:

$$\frac{A_1}{A_0} = 1 + \sum_i s_i \dot{p}_i \tag{10.5}$$

where $s_i = p_{0i}\gamma_i / \sum_i p_{0i}\gamma_i$. The term B_1/B_0 simplifies to:

$$\frac{B_1}{B_0} = \prod (p_{1i}/p_{0i})^{\beta_i} \tag{10.6}$$

This is a weighted geometric mean of price relatives and can be expressed in terms of proportionate changes.

10.1.3 Equivalent Incomes

The distributional effects of price changes can be examined using the distribution of equivalent incomes. Equivalent income is defined as the value of income (total expenditure), m_e, which, at some reference set of prices, p_r, gives the same utility as the actual income level; see chapter 4. In terms of the indirect utility function, m_e is therefore defined by the equation:

$$V(p_r, m_e) = V(p, m) \tag{10.7}$$

Using the expenditure function, $m_e = E(p_r, V(p, m))$, and for the linear expenditure system:

$$m_e = A_r + \frac{B_r(m - A)}{B} \tag{10.8}$$

Expanding the terms in A and B gives:

$$m_e = \sum_i p_{ri}\gamma_i + \left\{ \prod_i \left(\frac{p_{ri}}{p_i} \right)^{\beta_i} \right\} \left\{ m - \sum_j p_j\gamma_j \right\} \tag{10.9}$$

The effect on welfare of a change in prices and income can then be measured in terms of a change in equivalent incomes, from m_{0e} to m_{1e}, where, as before, the indices 0 and 1 refer to pre-change and post-change values respectively. Given observations on individual households from a cross-sectional household budget survey, a complete distribution of equivalent incomes can be obtained. Measures of inequality can be obtained using values of m_{0e} and m_{1e}, allowing the distributional effects to be examined for different degrees of inequality aversion.

Consider the use of pre-change prices as reference prices, so that $p_{ri} = p_{0i}$ for all i. Substitution into equation (10.9) shows immediately that pre-change equivalent incomes are the actual incomes, and thus $m_{0e} = m$. Equivalent incomes after the change in prices are given by:

$$m_{1e} = \sum_i p_{0i}\gamma_i + \left\{ \prod_i \left(\frac{p_{0i}}{p_{1i}} \right)^{\beta_i} \right\} \left\{ m - \sum_j p_{1j}\gamma_j \right\} \tag{10.10}$$

This can be written as:

$$m_{1e} = A_0 \left[1 + \frac{B_0}{B_1} \left(\frac{m}{A_0} - \frac{A_1}{A_0} \right) \right] \tag{10.11}$$

Comparison with equation (10.4) shows that when the reference prices are equal to the pre-change prices, the post-change equivalent income is the value of actual income after the change less the value of the equivalent variation; that is, $m_{1e} = m - EV$.

10.2 Monopoly and Prices

The previous section has shown how the welfare effects of price changes can be evaluated. This section considers the specification of price changes in the context of monopoly. The term monopoly is, as mentioned earlier, meant to denote the absence of competition, rather than a single firm in a market. In what follows, the subscript i, denoting the good, is dropped for convenience. The actual price of the good is treated as the monopoly price, p_m, throughout, and if p_c denotes the competitive price, then by definition:

$$\dot{p} = \frac{p_m}{p_c} - 1 \qquad (10.12)$$

In order to obtain the appropriate values of $\dot{p}_i$, it is necessary to have an independent expression for p_m/p_c. This is considered in the following subsection.

10.2.1　Identical Marginal Costs

Suppose that all firms in a given industry maximise profits and have the same marginal cost, mc, whether they are competitive or monopolists. This assumption requires that marginal cost is independent of output or market conditions, and implies that the competitive price, p_c, is equal to the value of the marginal cost to the monopolistic firms. Hence, (10.12) can be rewritten:

$$\dot{p} = \frac{p_m}{mc} - 1 \qquad (10.13)$$

Suppose also that all firms in an industry charge the same price for a homogeneous good, and that the kth firm perceives that it faces a demand elasticity of η_k. Assuming that the firm maximises profits, the standard relationship between price and marginal revenue gives:

$$mc_k = p_m \left(1 + \frac{1}{\eta_k} \right) \qquad (10.14)$$

The kth firm's elasticity, $\eta_k = (dx_k/x_k)/(dp/p)$, differs from the elasticity of demand facing the industry, $\eta = (dx/x)/(dp/p)$, because the former incorporates the firm's perception regarding the way in which other firms in the industry are thought to react to a change in the kth firm's output. From the basic definitions:

$$\eta_k = \eta \left(\frac{dx_k/x_k}{dx/dx} \right) \qquad (10.15)$$

Consider the denominator of (10.15). Writing $x = x_k + \sum_{j \neq k} x_j$, and totally differentiating gives:

$$dx = dx_k + \sum_{j \neq k} \frac{\partial x_j}{\partial x_k} dx_k \qquad (10.16)$$

Write $\sum_{j \neq k} \frac{\partial x_j}{\partial x_k} dx_k = \sum_{j \neq k} dx_j = d \sum_{j \neq k} x_j = dx_{(k)}$, and $s_k = x_k/x$, and noting that $x_{(k)}/x = (x - x_k)/x = 1 - s_k$, equation (10.16) can be rewritten as:

$$\frac{dx}{x} = s_k \frac{dx_k}{x_k} + (1 - s_k) \frac{dx_{(k)}}{x_{(k)}} \tag{10.17}$$

Defining $\alpha_k = \left(dx_{(k)}/x_{(k)} \right) / \left(dx_k/x_k \right)$ as the perceived elasticity of output of all other firms in the industry with respect to the kth firm's output, then:

$$\eta_k = \tau_k \eta \tag{10.18}$$

where:

$$\tau_k = \{s_k + (1 - s_k) \alpha_k\}^{-1} \tag{10.19}$$

Substituting this result in (10.12) gives an expression for marginal cost of:

$$mc_k = p_m \left(1 + \frac{1}{\tau_k \eta} \right) \tag{10.20}$$

On the further assumption that all the firms in any given industry have identical values of τ and hence, given the other assumptions, p_m/mc, (10.13) and (10.20) can be combined to give:

$$\dot{p} = \frac{1}{\tau |\eta| - 1} \tag{10.21}$$

Equation (10.21) can be used to find the proportional price increase over the price that would otherwise arise if the market were competitive. In the case of heterogeneous products, where the price is a decision variable, it can be shown that a very similar result applies but with τ interpreted in terms of conjectural variations regarding other firms' responses to price changes. For further discussion of this case, see Waterson (1984).

10.2.2 Different Marginal Costs

The previous subsection is based on the premise that the marginal cost is the same under monopoly as it would be under competition. However, it is possible that in industries where suppliers have some monopoly power, there are departures from cost minimisation as a result of organisational slack and X-inefficiency; see, for example, Frantz (1988). Consider the possibility that the monopolistic firm, whilst profit-maximising and thus producing a level of output at which its marginal revenue is equal to its marginal cost, has a marginal cost above the competitive marginal cost and thus competitive price, so that $p_c = \lambda mc$, where $0 < \lambda < 1$. In this case the price difference (10.12) has to be written as:

$$\dot{p} = \frac{p_m}{\lambda mc} - 1 \tag{10.22}$$

Under the assumption of profit maximisation, equation (10.20) still describes the relationship between marginal cost and marginal revenue for the firm, and substituting this into (10.22) yields:

$$\dot{p} = \frac{\tau |\eta| \left(\frac{1}{\lambda} - 1\right) + 1}{\tau |\eta| - 1} \tag{10.23}$$

Hence if $\lambda = 1$, the price changes are the same as in (10.21). Where $\lambda < 1$, as suggested, the price changes exceed those obtained under the assumption of identical marginal costs.

10.2.3   Computing Price Changes

The previous two subsections have derived expressions for $\dot{p}$ as functions of the own-price elasticity of demand. The present approach allows these elasticities to vary with the income (or total expenditure) of households, through variations in β_i and $p_i \gamma_i$. Hence two alternative approaches to the specification of the required $\dot{p}$s may be taken.

One approach would be to use just one set of $\dot{p}$s. For example, take the own-price elasticity of each good at the arithmetic mean household expenditure as a measure of the market elasticity, η. The resulting set of values of $\dot{p}$ could then be applied to all households. Alternatively, the assumption may be made that it is possible to model the economy as if each income (or total expenditure) group operates in a different market for each commodity.

For example, different income groups are to a certain extent concentrated in different urban districts or in different regions, serviced by local monopolists. Also, different income groups purchase goods which differ in their quality and thus in price. In this case a separate set of price changes can be applied to each income group. The following analysis examines the implications of adopting both approaches.

A problem is raised by the lack of information about the values of τ and λ. In addition, a further problem facing all researchers in this area is that, with the kind of commodity grouping available in the household expenditure survey, the estimated own-price elasticities are relatively low; indeed, they are all numerically less than unity. Using the limited information that is available about orders of magnitude for τ and λ in some industries, the use of either (10.21) or (10.23) does not result in positive values of $\dot{p}$. Faced with this awkward problem, the following analysis investigates the use of a range of values of τ, where, given the absence of *a priori* information, the same value is used for each commodity and income group. The lowest value of τ used (which is imposed purely by the need to have positive price changes) is 45; this must be regarded as a combination of an arbitrary adjustment of the low price elasticities and the effect of the conjectural variation term. This would be very worrying if it were required to measure the absolute value of the welfare loss from monopoly, where the absolute values of $\dot{p}$ would play a crucial role. In the present context, emphasis is on the relative welfare losses, so that this adjustment may not be regarded as too serious; indeed, the empirical results reveal little sensitivity to the value used. However, in view of the high size of this coefficient, it was found that the further use of sensible orders of magnitude for λ had very little effect on the results. Hence, only the use of (10.21) is reported below.

10.3 Empirical Results

The use of the 1993 Household Expenditure Survey to obtain the required parameter values of the LES for each income group is described in detail in Creedy and Martin (1997), following the approach set out in chapter 5.

Households were divided into 30 total expenditure groups, and information is available about the expenditure of almost 8,000 households on 16 commodity groups. A problem in estimating the LES is that a suitable value of the Frisch (1959) parameter, ξ, is required for each total expenditure group. Although it was possible to be guided by several independent studies, the precise values used must be regarded as having a substantial arbitrary element. For this reason, sensitivity analyses are reported. Three separate sets of values of ξ were used; in each case the absolute value is assumed to fall as total expenditure rises. The 'low', 'middle' and 'high' values indicated in the tables refer not only to the absolute values but also to the degree of variation with total expenditure.

10.3.1   Equivalent Variations

Table 10.1 shows the ratio of the equivalent variation to total expenditure for each total expenditure group. This ratio is the appropriate measure in this context, since it gives the proportional increase in equivalent income, when moving from the competitive to the monopolistic case. In obtaining the values in Table 10.1, the own-price elasticities obtained for each total expenditure group were used in computing the required values of $\dot{p}$. For each set of variations in ξ, results are given for three alternative values of τ. It can be seen that the ratios generally increase as ξ increases, and the difference between the ratios for high- and low-income groups is only slightly larger as ξ increases. For the higher variation in ξ, it was necessary to set the minimum value of τ higher than in the other cases, in order to generate positive price differences.

Table 10.2 shows the effects of using a single set of $\dot{p}$s in order to compute the compensating variations, as explained in the previous section. As expected, these show a smoother variation in the ratios of the equivalent variation to total expenditure, compared with Table 10.1. Both tables indicate a systematic reduction in the ratio as total expenditure rises. These ratios would be the same for each income group only if the proportional change in the price of each commodity group were the same for each commodity

Table 10.1: Ratio of Equivalent Variation to Expenditure

| | | Low ξ | | | Middle ξ | | | High ξ | |
No.	$\tau = 45$	55	65	45	55	65	55	60	65
1	1.247	1.298	1.329	1.396	1.458	1.496	2.241	2.246	2.251
2	2.179	1.964	1.887	6.392	2.937	2.493	10.755	6.094	4.864
3	1.530	1.530	1.536	2.084	1.914	1.864	3.477	3.213	3.065
4	1.272	1.316	1.343	1.502	1.539	1.564	2.438	2.417	2.405
5	1.185	1.233	1.264	1.368	1.424	1.458	2.207	2.208	2.211
6	1.110	1.162	1.195	1.249	1.318	1.360	1.989	2.007	2.021
7	1.111	1.162	1.193	1.256	1.323	1.363	1.995	2.011	2.024
8	1.108	1.157	1.187	1.266	1.327	1.365	2.012	2.023	2.033
9	1.073	1.121	1.151	1.221	1.282	1.319	1.928	1.940	1.951
10	1.060	1.106	1.136	1.207	1.266	1.302	1.894	1.906	1.916
11	1.044	1.091	1.121	1.180	1.240	1.278	1.835	1.849	1.861
12	1.066	1.111	1.140	1.209	1.266	1.301	1.870	1.881	1.890
13	1.067	1.111	1.138	1.214	1.268	1.301	1.865	1.873	1.880
14	1.053	1.096	1.123	1.196	1.249	1.281	1.824	1.832	1.840
15	1.042	1.084	1.110	1.183	1.233	1.264	1.790	1.797	1.803
16	1.032	1.073	1.098	1.172	1.220	1.249	1.759	1.765	1.770
17	1.025	1.064	1.089	1.168	1.211	1.238	1.737	1.741	1.744
18	1.023	1.059	1.082	1.173	1.209	1.232	1.729	1.727	1.727
19	1.028	1.060	1.081	1.200	1.219	1.235	1.749	1.735	1.728
20	1.063	1.082	1.096	1.344	1.281	1.272	1.899	1.832	1.796
21	1.160	1.134	1.131	2.797	1.486	1.371	2.732	2.214	2.027
22	1.044	1.055	1.065	1.365	1.251	1.232	1.803	1.730	1.692
23	0.952	0.981	0.999	1.082	1.102	1.118	1.481	1.478	1.477
24	1.023	1.024	1.030	1.382	1.211	1.181	1.659	1.594	1.559
25	0.990	0.994	1.001	1.269	1.153	1.134	1.520	1.479	1.457
26	0.891	0.916	0.933	0.982	1.004	1.019	1.264	1.267	1.269
27	0.862	0.887	0.903	0.936	0.959	0.975	1.176	1.181	1.184
28	0.857	0.870	0.880	0.948	0.941	0.945	1.113	1.111	1.110
29	0.707	0.736	0.754	0.717	0.753	0.775	0.855	0.864	0.872
30	1.000	1.000	1.000	1.000	1.000	1.000	1.000	1.000	1.000

Table 10.2: Ratio of Equivalent Variation to Expenditure: Uniform Price Effects

Group	Low ξ $\tau = 45$	65	Middle ξ 45	65	High ξ 55	65
1	1.555	1.544	1.593	1.563	1.605	1.605
2	1.500	1.486	1.544	1.507	1.555	1.555
3	1.459	1.446	1.501	1.465	1.512	1.512
4	1.432	1.420	1.472	1.437	1.482	1.482
5	1.409	1.397	1.447	1.414	1.457	1.457
6	1.390	1.380	1.426	1.395	1.435	1.435
7	1.377	1.366	1.414	1.383	1.423	1.423
8	1.362	1.351	1.399	1.367	1.407	1.407
9	1.347	1.337	1.382	1.352	1.390	1.390
10	1.333	1.323	1.366	1.337	1.374	1.374
11	1.321	1.312	1.353	1.325	1.360	1.360
12	1.311	1.300	1.342	1.314	1.349	1.349
13	1.298	1.287	1.328	1.300	1.334	1.334
14	1.286	1.276	1.315	1.288	1.320	1.320
15	1.273	1.263	1.301	1.275	1.306	1.306
16	1.261	1.252	1.288	1.263	1.293	1.293
17	1.249	1.240	1.274	1.250	1.279	1.279
18	1.237	1.228	1.261	1.238	1.265	1.265
19	1.226	1.217	1.249	1.227	1.253	1.253
20	1.214	1.205	1.235	1.214	1.238	1.238
21	1.200	1.192	1.220	1.200	1.223	1.223
22	1.185	1.178	1.203	1.185	1.206	1.206
23	1.171	1.164	1.186	1.170	1.189	1.189
24	1.155	1.149	1.168	1.154	1.171	1.171
25	1.138	1.133	1.150	1.138	1.152	1.152
26	1.122	1.117	1.131	1.121	1.133	1.133
27	1.103	1.099	1.110	1.102	1.112	1.112
28	1.079	1.077	1.084	1.078	1.085	1.085
29	1.047	1.046	1.048	1.046	1.049	1.049
30	1.000	1.000	1.000	1.000	1.000	1.000

and income group. This suggests that monopoly has a larger impact on the lower income groups, and therefore an inequality increasing effect. A further indication of this effect can be obtained by examining the distribution of equivalent incomes.

10.3.2 Equivalent Incomes

As explained in section 10.1, it is possible to calculate, for each household in the Household Expenditure Survey, values of equivalent income for the (counterfactual) competitive case and the monopoly case. Using the competitive case as the set of reference prices, the initial equivalent income is total expenditure, and the monopoly equivalent income is expenditure less the equivalent variation. In calculating these values, each household was first assigned to its appropriate total expenditure group, and all households in the same group were assumed to have the same preferences. The distribution of equivalent incomes was then used to calculate a range of inequality measures. Atkinson's inequality measure, for alternative values of the inequality aversion coefficient, ε, was obtained in each case. Furthermore, values of the extended Gini measure, $G\left(v\right)$, were obtained, where the coefficient, v, is equivalent to an inequality aversion coefficient and $v = 2$ corresponds to the standard and better-known Gini measure.

Alternative inequality measures are given in Table 10.3, where the first column gives the value of ε and the corresponding value of v, not shown in the table, is $1 + \varepsilon$. The measures for the expenditure distributions (corresponding to the 'pre-change' prices) are show in Table 10.5; these correspond to the distribution of equivalent income in the competitive case. The percentage changes compared with competition are given in Table 10.4. These results demonstrate that monopoly is associated with greater inequality.

One way to view these changes in inequality is in terms of the corresponding social welfare function that is associated with the use of the inequality measures. Although the Atkinson and Gini measures of inequality are related to very different types of value judgement, they are both associated with the same abbreviated form of social welfare function. If I denotes inequality (either A or G), then social welfare per person, W, can be expressed in terms of arithmetic mean income, $\bar{m}$, and I using:

$$W = \bar{m}\,(1 - I) \tag{10.24}$$

Hence the marginal rate of substitution between $\bar{m}$ and I is given by:

$$\left. \frac{d\bar{m}}{dI} \right|_W = \frac{\bar{m}}{1 - I} \tag{10.25}$$

and an x per cent increase in inequality is equivalent to a percentage increase in arithmetic mean income of $xI/\,(1 - I)$. For example, if $I = 0.1$ and inequality increases by 3 per cent, this is equivalent to a reduction in $\bar{m}$ of 0.33 per cent. For a higher initial inequality of 0.3, associated with a higher aversion to inequality, the same increase in inequality is associated with a corresponding reduction in $\bar{m}$ of 1.29 per cent.

10.4   Consumers' Surplus Measures

This section briefly describes the consumers' surplus method of measuring the welfare loss due to monopoly used in Creedy and Dixon (1998), and obtains comparable results using the 1993 HES. There are well-known problems associated with using this type of surplus measure as an approximation to a welfare loss. For example, Kay (1983, p.323-4) showed how the surplus measure can be regarded as an approximation to a welfare measure based on equivalent variations only if all the cross-price elasticities are zero. This is clearly violated; see also chapter 3 above. It is therefore useful to compare the exact welfare measures presented above with those obtained using the surplus measure.

The net loss of consumers' surplus, B, is measured using the standard result that the area of the loss triangle is half the price difference multiplied by the reduction in the quantity demanded. Hence:

$$B = (p_m - p_c)\,(q_c - q_m)\,/2 \tag{10.26}$$

Table 10.3: Inequality Measures of Equivalent Income

| | | Low Frisch | | |
| | $\tau = 45$ | | $\tau = 65$ | |
ε	$A(\varepsilon)$	$G(v)$	$A(\varepsilon)$	$G(v)$
0.1	0.0210	0.0622	0.0207	0.0617
0.4	0.0838	0.1993	0.0827	0.1977
0.7	0.1462	0.2921	0.1442	0.2899
1.3	0.2679	0.4115	0.2646	0.4088
1.6	0.3259	0.4527	0.3221	0.4499
		Middle Frisch		
	$\tau = 45$		$\tau = 65$	
ε	$A(\varepsilon)$	$G(v)$	$A(\varepsilon)$	$G(v)$
0.1	0.0214	0.0629	0.0209	0.062
0.4	0.0854	0.2014	0.0834	0.1987
0.7	0.1488	0.295	0.1455	0.2913
1.3	0.2723	0.4151	0.2667	0.4106
1.6	0.3310	0.4564	0.3246	0.4517
		High Frisch		
	$\tau = 55$		$\tau = 65$	
ε	$A(\varepsilon)$	$G(v)$	$A(\varepsilon)$	$G(v)$
0.1	0.0213	0.0628	0.0211	0.0624
0.4	0.0851	0.2011	0.0841	0.1997
0.7	0.1484	0.2946	0.1467	0.2927
1.3	0.2716	0.4146	0.2687	0.4122
1.6	0.3302	0.4559	0.3269	0.4534

Table 10.4: Percentage Changes in Inequality

	Low Frisch				
	$\tau = 45$			$\tau = 65$	
ε	$A(\varepsilon)$	$G(v)$		$A(\varepsilon)$	$G(v)$
0.1	3.96	2.47	1.1	2.48	1.65
0.4	3.97	2.26	1.4	2.61	1.44
0.7	3.84	2.06	1.7	2.41	1.29
1.3	3.56	1.86	2.3	2.28	1.19
1.6	3.36	1.75	2.6	2.16	1.12
	Middle Frisch				
	$\tau = 45$			$\tau = 65$	
ε	$A(\varepsilon)$	$G(v)$		$A(\varepsilon)$	$G(v)$
0.1	5.94	3.62		3.47	2.14
0.4	5.96	3.34		3.47	1.95
0.7	5.68	3.07		3.34	1.78
1.3	5.26	2.75		3.09	1.63
1.6	4.98	2.58		2.95	1.53
	High Frisch				
	$\tau = 55$			$\tau = 65$	
ε	$A(\varepsilon)$	$G(v)$		$A(\varepsilon)$	$G(v)$
0.1	5.45	3.46		4.46	2.80
0.4	5.58	3.18		4.34	2.46
0.7	5.40	2.94		4.19	2.27
1.3	4.99	2.62		3.87	2.03
1.6	4.73	2.47		3.68	1.91

Table 10.5: Expenditure Distributions

ε	$A(\varepsilon)$	v	$G(v)$
0.1	0.0202	1.1	0.0607
0.4	0.0806	1.4	0.1949
0.7	0.1408	1.7	0.2862
1.3	0.2587	2.3	0.404
1.6	0.3153	2.6	0.4449

The first term in (10.26) is Mp_m, where M is the Lerner (1934) index of monopoly power, M, defined as:

$$M_i = \frac{p_{m,i} - mc_i}{p_{m,i}} \tag{10.27}$$

The second term in parentheses in (10.26) can be expressed in terms of the own-price elasticity of demand, η, approximated by:

$$\eta = \frac{(q_m - q_c)}{(p_m - p_c)} \frac{p_m}{q_m} \tag{10.28}$$

Equation (10.28) assumes that the difference between the actual and competitive amounts are relatively small so that the numerator in each of the percentage change terms may be written as either the competitive amount or the monopoly amount. Substituting Mp_m for $p_m - p_c$ in (10.28) and rearranging gives $q_m - q_c = \eta M q_m$. Hence:

$$B = M^2 \eta \left(p_m q_m\right) /2 \tag{10.29}$$

Using $M = -\eta^{-1}$, this gives:

$$B = -\frac{p_m q_m}{2\eta} \tag{10.30}$$

Aggregating the welfare loss on each item of expenditure and expressing it as a proportion of the total expenditure on all n commodities gives a total welfare loss, L, of:

$$L = -\frac{1}{2} \sum_{i=1}^{n} \frac{w_i}{\eta_i} \tag{10.31}$$

where w_i is the ratio of expenditure on the ith commodity to total expenditure. The relative burden of monopoly for (say) a low-income household, L_L, relative to that of a high-income household, L_H, can thus be calculated using (10.31). Results are reported in Table 10.6. It can be seen that the relative values are not substantially different from those reported above.

Table 10.6: Consumer Surplus Measures

Group	Expenditure	Low ξ	Middle ξ	High ξ
1	10519	1.466	1.657	2.343
2	15247	1.763	2.019	2.862
3	18984	1.591	1.834	2.612
4	22272	1.465	1.689	2.405
5	25475	1.398	1.612	2.291
6	28590	1.340	1.540	2.177
7	31826	1.334	1.536	2.167
8	34793	1.320	1.524	2.147
9	38131	1.283	1.479	2.073
10	41517	1.264	1.457	2.032
11	44633	1.249	1.435	1.988
12	47759	1.263	1.449	1.996
13	51057	1.257	1.440	1.973
14	54101	1.240	1.418	1.931
15	57405	1.224	1.396	1.890
16	60685	1.208	1.376	1.850
17	64235	1.195	1.357	1.812
18	67712	1.182	1.340	1.777
19	71230	1.173	1.326	1.746
20	75325	1.169	1.319	1.722
21	79843	1.168	1.315	1.700
22	84968	1.128	1.262	1.612
23	90492	1.082	1.203	1.517
24	97495	1.081	1.196	1.486
25	104570	1.053	1.157	1.415
26	112638	1.005	1.095	1.316
27	122786	0.973	1.049	1.235
28	136429	0.934	0.995	1.139
29	158799	0.830	0.865	0.949
30	211695	1.000	1.000	1.000

10.5 Conclusions

The results of this chapter suggest that, whatever the size of the absolute welfare loss due to monopoly, there may be a substantial effect on the distribution of welfare. Nevertheless, the results must be viewed with much caution as they rest, as does much applied microeconomics, on strong assumptions. The analysis has also been restricted to a partial equilibrium framework. Hence the general equilibrium question of the effect of monopoly on employment levels and factor incomes has been ignored as have been issues to do with the distribution of monopoly profits. However, the latter is likely to reinforce the main conclusions.

Chapter 11

Carbon Taxation and Welfare

Recognition of the adverse effects of carbon dioxide emissions, resulting mainly from the combustion of fossil fuels, has led to proposals for non-market mechanisms such as regulation and market mechanisms such as tradable emissions permits and carbon taxes, in order to reduce emissions. Market methods are usually preferred in terms of efficiency and the carbon tax is deemed as being the easiest to implement and monitor. Owen (1992, p.4) compared carbon taxes with other instruments. Pearce (1991) provided a summary of the advantages and disadvantages of a carbon tax; and Dower and Zimmerman (1992) compared the merits of carbon taxes and tradable emission permits.

A carbon tax would affect the price of fossil fuels and thus consumer prices, both directly for fuels and indirectly for manufactured goods. These price changes would alter the levels of final demand, and therefore fossil fuel use and aggregate carbon dioxide emissions. This chapter investigates the orders of magnitude of a carbon tax required to reduce carbon dioxide emissions in Australia such that the Toronto Target is met; this requires a reduction in emissions of 20 per cent of 1988 levels by 2005. It also examines the distributional implications of carbon taxation where allowance is made for consumer responses to price changes and the indirect price effects of taxes.

The approach follows that of Symons *et al.* (1994) for the UK. However, a different type of demand system is used to obtain the many demand elasticities needed. The method focuses on the reduction in emissions resulting entirely from consumer demand responses. This chapter also examines the implications of changes in intermediate requirements in the production process, that is, a change in the input-output matrix. The analysis comprises three stages, which are outlined in the following subsection. The individual components of each stage are more fully explained in section 11.1. Section 11.2 provides information regarding calibration of the model. The simulation results are discussed in section 11.3, with the effects of allowing for technological substitution considered in section 11.4.

11.0.1   The Three Stage Process

The first stage is to apply a carbon tax. If the carbon tax is shifted forward to consumers, it increases the price of goods in proportion to their carbon content. These price changes can be modelled as being equivalent to a set of indirect taxes on consumer goods. The assumption of full shifting is of course very strong, requiring competitive markets and constant returns, but is the standard assumption used in partial equilibrium analyses of indirect taxes. The analysis does not allow for general equilibrium effects, such as changes in factor prices and (pre-tax) goods prices resulting from a carbon tax. If c_i is the carbon dioxide intensity for commodity group i and α is the tax on carbon dioxide emissions (measured in dollars per tonne of carbon dioxide), it is possible to calculate the equivalent *ad valorem* tax rate on the ith commodity group, t_i, measured as a percentage of the tax-exclusive value of the commodity group, using:

$$t_i = \alpha c_i \qquad (11.1)$$

The second stage is to calculate the demand response of consumers to the price changes. These responses are determined using the method described in chapter 5. The approach assumes no labour supply responses. New expenditure levels are calculated for each household from which the amount of indirect tax paid on all goods is subtracted, giving total net consumption. Measures of inequality and progressivity are then based on the change in net consumption.

The final stage is to calculate the new levels of aggregate demand for each commodity group in order to determine the reduction in carbon dioxide emissions. Hence the reduction in emissions is obtained at the last of the three stages and, because of the complexity involved in each of the three stages, it is not possible to calculate directly the value of α that would achieve a specified reduction in emission. This requires an iterative search procedure involving the use of an arbitrary initial value of α and then a gradual process of adjustment involving the repeated application of the three stages until the desired reduction in emissions is produced.

The first and third stages described above use the same input-output matrix, so that carbon dioxide reductions result only from consumer substitution. That is, it is assumed that there is no substitution in production and all substitution falls on the demand side. This assumption is made due to the lack of information on, and widely varying estimates of, possible substitutions in production; see Owen (1992, p.5). However, it is likely that there would be a relatively large amount of substitution in production if a carbon tax were imposed in Australia. Hence, it is of interest to calculate the potential effect on emissions of specified changes in the input-output matrix.

11.1 The Analytical Framework

11.1.1 Carbon Tax and Price Changes

A carbon tax is imposed on the carbon content of fuels used in production and consumption, rather than carbon dioxide emissions, and hence the majority of studies specify carbon taxes in terms of dollars per tonne of carbon. However, as carbon content and carbon dioxide emissions are directly proportional, a carbon tax can be converted to a tax on carbon dioxide emissions merely by multiplying the former by the relative elemental weight of carbon to carbon dioxide. Carbon has a weight of 12 and oxygen a weight of 16, therefore CO_2 has a total weight of 44 and the relative weight of carbon to carbon dioxide is approximately 0.272727. For example, a carbon tax of \$100 per tonne of carbon is equal to a tax of \$27.27 per tonne of carbon dioxide emissions.

To calculate the set of equivalent indirect taxes according to equation (11.1) it is necessary to have the carbon tax specified as a tax on carbon dioxide emissions. It is also required to know the carbon dioxide intensities, c_i, of the commodity groups involved. Carbon dioxide emissions are largely the result of the combustion of fossil fuels and arise from the production and consumption of goods. When calculating the emissions from consumption it is appropriate to consider only domestic consumption; final demand figures for fossil fuels are therefore adjusted to exclude exports and the stockbuilding of fuels. Data on carbon dioxide emissions resulting from sources other than the combustion of fossil fuels are not available for Australia. In determining emissions from production, it is not enough to consider only final products; gross output, allowing for inter-industry trade, must be considered.

Define the following variables, where vectors are columns and coefficients are in value terms:

e is the k-vector of CO_2 emission per unit of fossil fuel use (for k fossil-fuels).

P is the $(n \times k)$ matrix of household fuel requirements per unit of final demand, for each producing sector, and for each fossil fuel.

Z is the $(n \times n)$ diagonal matrix of weights, to exclude from consideration the export and stock building of fuels.

C is the $(n \times k)$ matrix of production fuel requirements per unit of total demand, for each producing sector, and for each fossil fuel.

A is the $(n \times n)$ matrix of technological coefficients, relating the inputs to each producing sector to the total outputs by the sectors.

y is the n-vector of final demand for each sector.

Carbon dioxide emissions can be expressed as a weighted sum of final demands. Following Proops *et al.* (1993, p.127), total emissions, E, are:

$$E = \left[e'P'Z + e'C' \left(I - A \right)^{-1} \right] y \qquad (11.2)$$

where a prime indicates transposition. The vector in square brackets in equation (11.2) is the required vector of $c_i s$, which is precisely the information required to calculate a set of indirect taxes according to equation (11.1).

11.1.2 Demand Responses and Tax Revenue

From the price changes it is possible to calculate the demand responses of consumers using demand elasticities which vary with household income. From the new demands, and using the equivalent tax-inclusive indirect rate, it is possible to determine the amount of indirect tax paid and hence net total expenditure. Let m denote the total expenditure of a household, consisting of expenditure on each of n commodities, where consumption of the ith commodity is denoted x_i $(i = 1, ..., n)$. If prices are denoted by p_i $(i = 1, ..., n)$, the demand function for good i is:

$$x_i = x_i \left(p_i, ..., p_n \mid m \right) \qquad (11.3)$$

If $\dot{p}_j = dp_j/p_j$, and η_{ij} is the cross-price elasticity of demand for good i with respect to a change in the price of good j, $(dx_i/x_i) / (dp_j/p_j)$, the new level of expenditure, m_i, resulting from price changes is given by:

$$m_i = p_i x_i \left(1 + \dot{p}_i + \sum_j \eta_{ij} \dot{p}_j \right) \qquad (11.4)$$

As explained above, the price changes are considered to result from a commodity tax equivalent to the carbon tax. Suppose as before that t_i denotes the tax-exclusive consumption tax rate on good i, so the tax-inclusive price of the good is $1 + t_i$ multiplied by the tax-exclusive price. Hence the introduction of a consumption tax translates into a proportional change in the price. The equivalent tax-inclusive rate is given by $t_i / (1 + t_i)$. Hence, the tax revenue from the ith good after the price change is given by R_i, where:

$$R_i = \left(\frac{t_i}{1 + t_i} \right) m_i \qquad (11.5)$$

The new revenue arising from changes to the indirect tax rates can therefore be obtained from (11.4) to obtain m_i and then using equation (11.5).

11.1.3   Demand Elasticities

The number of demand elasticities required is obviously very large. In this chapter the 1984 Australian Household Expenditure Survey is used. Even with the high level of aggregation of the data, with 14 commodity groups and 30 income groups, it is necessary to determine almost 6,000 own and cross-price elasticities. Because of the paucity of household expenditure data in Australia, it is not possible to produce the type of econometric estimates for different population groups, as used by Symons et al. (1994). The method used in this chapter instead follows that described in chapter 5. This method has the advantage of not requiring price information but has the corresponding disadvantage that it uses price elasticities based on theoretical restrictions rather than observed responses to price changes. A brief summary of the process is given here.

The first stage in calculating the elasticities is to obtain the total expenditure elasticities for each commodity group and level of total expenditure. The total expenditure elasticities are obtained by using a matrix with K rows, for the total expenditure levels, such that each row contains the budget shares for each of the n commodity groups. The n elasticities for the kth total expenditure group can be found using the approximation:

$$e_i = 1 + \frac{\triangle w_i / w_i}{\triangle m / m}$$

where the k subscripts have been omitted for convenience and, for example, $\triangle w_i$ denotes the change in the budget share of the ith commodity when moving from total expenditure group k to group $k + 1$.

Having determined expenditure weights and the total expenditure elasticities, it is possible to calculate price elasticities by proceeding on the assumption that preferences are additive. Frisch (1959) demonstrated that the price elasticities can be written for $i \neq j$ as:

$$\eta_{ij} = -e_i w_j \left(1 + e_j / \xi\right) \tag{11.6}$$

and for $i = j$ as:

$$\eta_{ii} = e_i/\xi - e_i w_i \left(1 + e_i/\xi\right) \qquad (11.7)$$

where ξ is the total expenditure elasticity of the marginal utility of total expenditure, usually referred to as the Frisch parameter. These expressions automatically satisfy the homogeneity and additivity restrictions. Additive preferences imply that all goods are net substitutes, so that when p_j rises the compensated demand for good i rises.

The expressions (11.6) and (11.7) allow the price elasticities to be calculated using only household budget data. Budget data provide information about the budget shares w_i and hence the total expenditure elasticities, e_i, but it is necessary to specify the Frisch parameter using extraneous information.

The demand responses, or changes in total expenditure, calculated using the above method are in value terms. The input-output framework is also in value terms, so in order to calculate the new level of emissions after the imposition of a carbon tax it is necessary to convert the changes in total expenditure to constant price equivalents. The resulting levels of total expenditure are then fed back into equation (11.2) to determine the new level of carbon dioxide emissions.

11.1.4 The Simulation Approach

It would be possible to apply the three-stage procedure to individual households in the HES. However, this chapter has not obtained elasticities for different household types, because of the data limitations mentioned above, and instead uses a simulated population. The use of a simulated distribution of household incomes provides a sufficiently good description of the actual distribution, and avoids the need to deal with grossing up and other issues. Household incomes are simulated from a lognormal distribution, having a mean and variance of logarithms of 10 and 0.5 respectively, which provides a good approximation to the Australian household income distribution in 1984; see Creedy (1992).

Table 11.1: Income Tax Rates and Thresholds

Threshold	Marginal Tax Rate
4595	0.2667
12500	0.3000
19500	0.4600
28000	0.4733
35000	0.5533
35788	0.6000

An income tax structure is applied directly to incomes. A stylised transfer payment system is specified so that it is possible to consider the question of whether adjustments to transfer payments can offset the negative effects of a carbon tax. Transfer payments are modelled using a minimum income guarantee (MIG), such that if after-tax income falls below a minimum level then a transfer is paid to bring net income up to the minimum level.

For each household, an income level is simulated. The income tax structure is applied, and post-tax income is calculated. The 1984 income tax structure is taken directly from the Australian income tax schedule, and the income tax rates and thresholds used are given in Table 11.1. Post-tax income is adjusted, where appropriate, using the minimum income guarantee. This post-tax income gives the level of total expenditure, m. It is then possible to find to which expenditure group the household belongs, and therefore the appropriate set of income and price elasticities. In popular debates it is often argued that consumption taxes are regressive because the relatively rich save a higher proportion of disposable income. However, such savings are ultimately spent and will therefore incur the consumption tax, in addition to any interest-income tax. In the absence of an interest-income tax, the present value of tax payments is independent of the time pattern of consumption. The approach adopted here is therefore to ignore savings.

When a new indirect tax is introduced, the new levels of expenditure are calculated for each household using equation (11.4). From this information, the amount of indirect tax paid on each taxed good is determined using equation (11.5). This is then subtracted from each household's disposable income to find net consumption. Progressivity and income inequality measures can be calculated using net consumption to provide information regarding the distributional implications of changing the indirect tax structure. Basing these calculations on net consumption represents what is often referred to as a non-welfarist approach.

11.2 Calibrating the Model

First, it is necessary to determine the total level of carbon dioxide emissions, using equation (11.2), before a carbon tax is imposed. Cornwell and Creedy (1997) have calibrated this equation for Australia. The majority of the data are from two sources. Information on total energy consumption by industry and fuel type are given in ABARE (1990, Table C1, pp.78-90). Only the data for the financial year 1989-90 relating to the six primary fuels wood, bagasse, black coal, brown coal, oil and gas were used. The National Accounts Input-Output Tables for 1989-90 provide data on inter-industry flows in value terms; see ABS (1994, Table 5, microfiche and Table 11, pp.46-48). The 28-sector, as opposed to the 109-sector, classification was used as price changes and demand changes arising from a carbon tax need to be reconciled with the 14-commodity grouping of the HES data. Furthermore, the energy data are not available at a highly disaggregated level.

Secondly, information is required on household expenditure patterns and their elasticities, which determine demand changes resulting from changes in prices. Data from the 1984 Australian Household Expenditure Survey were used for expenditure by households on 14 different commodity groups, divided into 30 income categories. In calculating the price elasticities, it is appropriate to assume that the Frisch parameter varies with total expenditure. By experimenting with alternative hypothetical sets of combinations of ms and ξs, and using these to estimate alternative functional relationships, it was found that the following equation produced a set of values of ξ that follows the type of variation described by Frisch (1959, p.189):

$$log\,(-\xi) = 18.57 - 1.72 \log\,(m + 10575) \qquad (11.8)$$

This equation produces a set of Frisch values ranging approximately from -0.2 to -11.4. Both smaller and larger variations in the values with income were also considered. However, it was found that the general results were unaffected, and furthermore the differences in the absolute values of the inequality, progressivity and welfare measures reported below were minimal. Hence, this chapter reports only the results of using the Frisch values determined according to equation (11.8).

11.2.1 Commodity Groups

Once the input-output data have been used to obtain the pre-tax level of carbon dioxide emissions, they are used to calculate a set of indirect taxes equivalent to a particular carbon tax, using equation (11.1). These indirect taxes are implied price changes for the 28 input-output categories. However, the HES data are available only for 14 consumption categories, using a different classification form the 28 input-output sectors. It is necessary to translate the 28 price changes into 14 price changes so that demand responses can be calculated. The resulting set of total expenditure (final demand) changes must then be translated back to the 28-sector classification so that the new level of carbon dioxide emissions can be determined.

For the process of translating the 28 price changes into 14 price changes, for sectors where there is only one of the 28-sectors related to one of the 14-groups the price change is obviously translated directly. For the cases where there are several 28-sector classifications relating to one 14-group classification, the price change for the group category is taken as a weighted average of the related sector price changes, with the weights being the proportional contribution to the sum of the final demands for those sectors. For groups 9 and 12 of the 14 groups there are no input-output sectors deemed appropriate and so the price changes in these two groups are assumed to be zero.

The 14-group price changes are then used to determine the demand responses of households as described above. Once the 14 demand changes are calculated it is necessary to translate these back up into the 28-sector classification in order to determine the final effect on the level of carbon dioxide emissions using equation (11.2). For all input-output sectors except 5 (beverages, tobacco products), 19 (water) and 26 (public administration, defence), the figure translated is that calculated for the corresponding HES group. For input-output sector 5, a weighted average of the demand response from HES groups 4 and 5 is used, where the weights are 0.65 and 0.35 (approximately the respective proportions of the two groups to the sum of their new levels of expenditure). For input-output sectors 19 and 26 there are no HES sectors considered appropriate, and thus it is assumed that there was no change in the level of demand for these sectors.

11.3 Simulation Results

There are three main issues of initial concern. First, what is the order of magnitude of a carbon tax required to reduce emissions in Australia such that the Toronto Target is met? Secondly, what is the distributional impact of such a tax? Thirdly, is it possibly to overcome the negative impact of a carbon tax by increasing transfer payments?

The calculation of the required carbon tax can only be achieved by a search process of trial and error, involving the repeated use of the above three-stage procedure until a value of α is found that generates the desired reduction in emissions. With a constant minimum income guarantee of \$8000, the carbon dioxide tax, the value of α, as in equation (11.1), required to reduce emissions in Australia by 20 per cent from the 1989/90 figures was found to be 0.113, which is A\$113 per tonne of carbon dioxide, or A\$414 (US\$306) per tonne of carbon. The equivalent set of indirect taxes for this level of carbon tax is given in Table 11.2, which also gives the ratio of post- to pre-tax demands. Symons *et al.* (1994, pp.23, 28) report that the required tax for the UK is US\$411 per tonne of carbon, which is considerably higher. It is not clear if the UK faces lower demand elasticities, or if the difference arises from the structure of inter-industry transactions.

Looking at Table 11.2, it is of interest to note for which sectors the price increases are the greatest. It is not surprising that fuel and power (2) faces by far the biggest increase. Combined with the fact that lower-income earners

Table 11.2: Indirect Tax Rates to Reduce Emissions by 20 per cent

	14-Sector HES Classifications	Tax Rate, t_i	Demand Ratio
1	Current housing costs	0.0440	0.9537
2	Fuel and power	1.3609	0.7335
3	Food	0.1030	0.9247
4	Alcoholic beverages	0.1069	0.8594
5	Tobacco	0.1069	0.9379
6	Clothing and footwear	0.0461	0.9009
7	Household furnishings & equipment	0.0726	0.8638
8	Household services	0.0226	0.9573
9	Medical care and health	0.0000	0.9509
10	Transport	0.0885	0.8609
11	Recreation	0.0834	0.8679
12	Personal care	0.0000	0.9454
13	Miscellaneous goods & services	0.0408	0.9017
14	Others	0.1660	0.7210

spend a higher proportion of their budget than higher-income earners on fuel and power, this suggests that a carbon tax is regressive. Furthermore, food (3) and tobacco (5), which also face relatively large price increases, also form a higher proportion of the budget of lower-income earners. Another factor to consider is that for goods on which lower-income earners spend a relatively higher proportion of their budget, the lower-income earners have relatively lower price elasticities compared with higher-income earners, and therefore have less scope for substitution. However, there are also sectors facing relatively large price increases on which lower-income earners spend proportionately less. The price increase for others (14) is the second largest after fuel and power, yet the proportion of total expenditure spent on this sector increases with income. This relationship is also true of recreation (10). For transport (10), the relationship is a humped shape. Therefore, although it appears that a carbon tax may well reduce the degree of progressivity and increase inequality, it is not unambiguous.

The distributional impact of the tax can be assessed using a variety of measures. The Gini measure is a very commonly used measure of inequality, and can be related to the famous Lorenz curve diagram which plots the proportion of people against the corresponding proportion of total income, when incomes are arranged in ascending order (the Gini measure is an area-based measure of the distance of the actual Lorenz curve from the diagonal line of equality). The Reynolds-Smolensky measure is an index of the redistributive impact of the tax system; it is obtained as the difference between the Gini inequality measures of pre-tax and post-tax income.

The Kakwani progressivity measure is a measure of the disproportionality of tax payments. It is also based on ideas relating to the Lorenz diagram. If, instead of plotting the proportion of total income against the corresponding proportion of people, a curve is plotted showing the proportion of total tax paid against the proportion of people (with people ranked in ascending order by pre-tax income), then a curve called the tax concentration curve is obtained. A tax concentration measure similar to the Gini inequality measure can be obtained for this curve. For a proportional tax system, the tax concentration curve obviously coincides with the Lorenz curve of pre-tax incomes. Hence the disproportionality of tax payments can be measured as the difference between the tax concentration measure and the Gini measure of pre-tax incomes.

The social welfare premium from progression is defined as the additional welfare from the tax structure, compared with the welfare from a proportional tax raising the same revenue, using the Gini-based social welfare function $\bar{m}(1-G)$ where $\bar{m}$ is the arithmetic mean value of m, and G is the Gini measure of inequality; for further information on alternative measures see Lambert (1993a, b) and Creedy (1996).

These measures were calculated, using a minimum income guarantee of \$8000, both before and after the carbon tax is introduced. The results are reported in Table 11.3. It can be seen from these results that the carbon tax reduces the degree of progressivity and has adverse distributional effects. For example, the Gini inequality measure increases by 2.16 per cent, the Kakwani progressivity measure decreases by 30.29 per cent and the Gini welfare premium decreases by 15.64 per cent. The effect of the carbon tax

Table 11.3: A Carbon Tax per Tonne C

Distributional Measures	Pre-carbon Tax	Post-carbon Tax
Gini measure of inequality	0.2778	0.2838
Kakwani measure of progressivity	0.2050	0.1429
Reynolds-Smolensky measure	0.1004	0.0944
Total tax ratio	0.3287	0.3977
Welfare premium from progression (/1000)	1.8779	1.5848

on the price of fuel and power is, therefore, driving the results. Alternative summary measures, not reported here, also gave similar results.

In analysing the distributional impact of a carbon tax to achieve the Toronto Target, Symons *et al.* (1994) gave results for the Gini measure of inequality and for three levels of inequality aversion (0.1, 1.0 and 10.0) for the Atkinson inequality measure. Regarding the Gini measure, not only are the absolute values for Australia less than for the UK, but also the increase in inequality of 2.16 per cent reported here is less than that of 2.92 per cent reported by Symons *et al.* (1994, p.32). This is consistent with the assumption that UK consumers are less able to substitute away from goods with high carbon contents than are Australian consumers, therefore the set of indirect taxes to achieve the Toronto Target level of emissions reduction would need to be higher for the UK than Australia, giving rise to the result that a carbon tax increases inequality proportionately more in the UK.

Atkinson measures are shown in Table 11.4. The welfare premium before the carbon tax is 1.8779. With a level of aversion of 0.1, as with the Gini measure, both the absolute values and the percentage increases in inequality are less for Australia than for the UK; the absolute values are less by a factor of approximately 1/2, and the percentage increases are 4.76 per cent and 6.62 per cent respectively. The same result holds with a level of aversion of 1.0. For Australia, the lower is the aversion parameter, the higher is the

Table 11.4: Inequality and the Welfare Premium

Inequality Aversion	Pre-carbon Tax Inequality	Post-carbon Tax Inequality	Welfare Premium (/1000)
0.1	0.0126	0.0132	0.1844
0.5	0.0607	0.0634	0.8646
0.8	0.0944	0.0985	1.3221
1.0	0.1158	0.1207	1.5842
1.2	0.1363	0.1420	1.8765
2.0	0.2094	0.2175	2.8622

percentage increase in inequality. This trend does not hold with the results obtained by Symons *et al.* (1994, p.32).

The above carbon tax involves a revenue-increasing change; the overall effective tax ratio increases from 0.3287 to 0.3977. It is of interest to see whether the negative effects of introducing a carbon tax can be overcome by using some of the extra revenue to increase transfer payments whilst still achieving the Toronto Target level of emissions reduction. If the minimum income guarantee is increased then this affects consumption patterns on top of the changes brought about by the tax, which will lead to a lessening in the reduction of emissions, given that fuel is a higher proportion of total expenditure of low-income groups. This is partially compensated by the fact that increasing the minimum income guarantee pushes lower earners into a higher income bracket, which means they then have higher elasticities, and so are able to substitute away from relatively heavily taxed carbon-intensive goods more easily. However, to increase the minimum income guarantee and meet the Toronto Target, the carbon tax rate also needs to be increased. But an increase in the carbon tax rate leads to a worsening effect on inequality and progressivity. The question is whether or not it is possible to reach a convergence such that the negative effects of the carbon tax are overcome whilst still attaining the target level of reductions and not reducing total revenue. The result is that it is possible to do so. For example, it was found that with a carbon dioxide tax of 0.15, which translates to a tax of A\$550 (US\$743) per tonne of carbon, and a minimum income guarantee of \$12000, inequality decreased, progressivity increased and the welfare premium increased, whilst carbon dioxide emissions were reduced by 21.6 per cent and total revenue actually increased. It would be possible to determine a tax rate and minimum income guarantee which reduces emissions by exactly 20 per cent and is also revenue neutral; however, the results are sufficient to demonstrate that the negative effect of a carbon taxation can be compensated by adjustments to transfer payments.

11.4 Technological Substitution

The above results assume that consumers bear all the substitution required to reduce emissions. Pearce (1991), in his review of carbon taxes, presented estimates of the levels of tax that would reduce emissions by roughly 20 per cent in each of the UK, the US and Norway, where allowance is made for long-run substitution in production. The average of the figures is US\$174 for the UK, US\$149 for the US, and US\$126 for Norway. For Australia, McDougall (1993, p.8) used a carbon tax of A\$80 (US\$59) per tonne of carbon, which he took from a study reported by the Industry Commission (1991, p.189). However, the tax allows for an unspecified amount of substitution in production. Despite the difficulties involved, it would be useful to have some idea of the orders of magnitude involved in allowing for substitution in production. One approach is to examine the changes to the input-output matrix that would be required to reduce emissions by approximately 20 per cent with a tax rate closer to the estimates summarised by Pearce (1991). These studies produced tax rates to achieve the Toronto Target that are approximately half the size of the A\$414 per tonne of carbon (0.113 carbon dioxide) tax rate reported above as being the level necessary to achieve the Target without technological substitution. Therefore, the distributional implications of a tax of A\$200 per tonne of carbon (a carbon dioxide tax of 0.05), were examined, along with the corresponding degree of technological substitution necessary to reduce emissions to the Toronto Target level.

There are limitless combinations of changes that would achieve the desired reduction in emissions. However, it is appropriate to consider the effects of a substitution in production away from fuels with high carbon contents and towards gas, along with a general reduction in all inputs used by industries producing high amounts of carbon dioxide. The following assumptions were therefore based on close study of the emissions and carbon contents per dollar in each industry, along with industries which experience high price changes resulting from a carbon tax, although the actual values are to some extent arbitrary. Suppose there is a 12 per cent reduction in the use of sectors (10), (11) and (12) as inputs to other sectors, a 25 per cent increase in the use of gas (18) as an input, and a 4 per cent decrease in the use of all inputs in production in sectors (2), (4), (5), (9) to (13), (17), (20), (23), (26), (27) and (28). It was found that emissions are reduced by 19.4 per cent with a carbon tax of A$200. Given that the time frame in which these changes would need to occur would be in the vicinity of 10-20 years, these rates are not excessive.

The distributional impact of a carbon dioxide tax of 0.05 with the above changes is that the Gini measure of inequality increases 0.9 per cent, the Kakwani progressivity measure decreases 14.39 per cent and the Gini-based welfare premium decreases 6.75 per cent. These figures are markedly less adverse than those for the tax of 0.113 where there was no allowance for substitution in production, which were 2.16, 30.29 and 15.64 per cent respectively. This result is expected, given that most of the reduction in emissions with the tax of 0.05 is attributed to substitution in production, not consumption. Indeed, it was calculated that of the 19.4 per cent decrease in emissions, 8.2 percentage points are attributed to changes in consumption.

11.5   Conclusions

This chapter has examined the orders of magnitude of a carbon tax required to reduce carbon dioxide emission in Australia such that the Toronto Target is met. It has also looked at the effects on inequality and progressivity of carbon taxation where allowance is made for both consumer responses to price changes and the indirect price effects of taxes. The approach was to model a carbon tax as a set of *ad valorem* taxes on commodity groups. Input-output data were required to calculate the appropriate tax rates, and HES data were used to determine consumers' responses to the price changes. However, given that assuming no substitution in production is unrealistic, this chapter also investigated the effect of allowing for substitution in production.

Although the order of magnitude of a carbon tax to reduce emissions in Australia by 20 per cent, assuming no technological substitution, is high at A\$414/US\$306 per tonne of carbon, it is less than that calculated by Symons *et al.* (1994) for the UK (US\$411). Furthermore,the distributional implications of the tax are also less adverse for Australia. Nevertheless, such comparisons need to be treated with caution given the differences in approach and types of data used.

The carbon tax involves an increase in total tax revenue and a reduction in the degree of progressivity, with an increase in inequality. However, it was found that transfer payments can be adjusted to compensate for the regressivity of a carbon tax without decreasing total revenue.

Bibliography

[1] ABARE (1990) *Projections of Energy Demand and Supply in Australia 1990-91 to 2004-05.* Canberra: Australian Government Publishing Service.

[2] Australian Bureau of Statistics (1994) *Australian National Accounts: Input-Output Tables 1989-90.* Catalogue no. 5209.0. Canberra: Australian Government Publishing Service.

[3] Ahmad, E. and Stern, N.H. (1984) The theory of tax reform and Indian indirect taxes. *Journal of Public Economics*, 25, pp. 259-289.

[4] Ahmad, E. and Stern, N.H. (1991) *The Theory and Practice of Tax Reform in Developing Countries.* Cambridge: Cambridge University Press.

[5] Allen, R.G.D. (1975) *Index Numbers in Theory and Practice.* London: Macmillan.

[6] Anderson, R.W. (1980) Some theory of inverse demand for applied demand analysis. *European Economic Review*, 14, pp. 281-290.

[7] Apps, P. and Savage, E. (1989) Labour supply, welfare rankings and the measurement of inequality. *Journal of Public Economics*, 47, pp. 336-364.

[8] Atkinson, A.B. (1970) On the measurement of inequality. *Journal of Economic Theory*, 2, pp. 244-263.

[9] Atkinson, A.B. and Stern, N.H. (1974) Pigou, taxation and public goods. *Review of Economic Studies*, 41, pp. 119-128.

[10] Atkinson, A.B. and Stiglitz, J.E. (1980) *Lectures in Public Economics*. New York: McGraw-Hill.

[11] Auerbach, A.J. (1985) The theory of excess burden and optimal taxation. In *Handbook of Public Economics,* vol. 1 (ed. by A.J. Auerbach and M. Feldstein), pp. 61-127. Amsterdam: Elsevier.

[12] Australian Taxation Office (1989) *Taxation Statistics 1987-88*. Canberra: Australian Government Publishing Service.

[13] Balk, B.M. (1995) Approximating a cost-of-living index from demand functions: a retrospect. *Economics Letters*, 49, pp. 147-155.

[14] Ballard, C.L. (1990) Marginal welfare cost calculations: differential analysis vs. balanced-budget analysis. *Journal of Public Economics*, 41, pp. 263-276.

[15] Ballard, C.L. and Fullerton, D. (1992) Distortionary taxation and the provision of public goods. *Journal of Economic Perspectives*, 6, pp. 117-131.

[16] Ballard, C.L., Showen J.B. and Whalley J. (1985) The total welfare cost of the United States tax system: a general equilibrium approach. *National Tax Journal*, 38, pp. 125-140.

[17] Banks, J., Blundell, R. and Lewbel, A. (1996) Tax reform and welfare measurement: do we need demand system estimation? *Economic Journal*, 106, pp. 1227-1241.

[18] Becht, M. (1995) The theory and estimation of individual and social welfare measures. *Journal of Economic Surveys*, 9, pp. 53-87.

[19] Besley, T.J. and Preston, I.P. (1988) Invariance and the axiomatics of income tax progression: a comment. *Bulletin of Economic Research*, 40, pp. 159-163.

[20] Blackorby, C. and Donaldson, D. (1988) Money metric utility: a harmless normalization? *Journal of Economic Theory.* 46, pp. 120-129.

[21] Blinder, A.S. and Esaki, H.Y. (1978) Macroeconomic activity and income distribution in the postwar United States. *Review of Economics and Statistics,* 60, pp.604-608.

[22] Blomquist, N.S. (1983) The effect of income taxation on the labour supply of married men in Sweden. *Journal of Public Economics,* 22, pp. 169-97.

[23] Blundell, R. (1988) Consumer demand behaviour: theory and empirical evidence–a survey. *Economic Journal,* 98, pp. 16-65.

[24] Blundell, R. (1992) Labour supply and taxation: a survey. *Fiscal Studies,* 13, pp. 15-40.

[25] Blundell, R., Pashardes, P. and Weber, G. (1993) What do we learn about consumer demand patterns from micro data? *American Economic Review,* 83, pp. 570-597.

[26] Blundell, R., Preston, I. and Walker, I. (eds) (1994) *The Measurement of Household Welfare.* Cambridge: Cambridge University Press.

[27] Bockstael, N.E. and McConnell, K.E. (1993) Public goods as characteristics of non-market commodities. *Economic Journal,* 103, pp. 1244-1257.

[28] Breslaw, J.A. and Smith, J.B. (1995) Measuring welfare changes when quantity is constrained. *Journal of Business and Economic Statistics,* 13, pp. 95-103.

[29] Broad, A. and Bacica, L. (1985) *The Incidence of Indirect Taxes,* Vol. 2. Wellington: Victoria University Press.

[30] Brown, J.A.C. and Deaton, A.S. (1973) Models of consumer behaviour. In *Surveys of Applied Economics,* Vol. I, pp. 177-268. London: Macmillan.

[31] Browning, E.K. (1976) The marginal cost of public funds. *Journal of Political Economy*, 84, pp. 283-298.

[32] Browning, E.K. (1985) A critical appraisal of Hausman's welfare cost estimates. *Journal of Political Economy*, 93, pp. 1025-1034.

[33] Browning, E.K. (1987) On the marginal welfare cost of taxation, *American Economic Review*, 77, pp. 11-23.

[34] Chipman, J.S. and Moore, J.C. (1980) Compensating variation, consumer's surplus, and welfare. *American Economic Review*, 70, pp. 933-949.

[35] Chisholm, A. (1993) Indirect taxation and consumption efficiency. In *Fightback: An Economic Assessment* (ed. by J. Head), pp. 309-350. Sydney: Australian Tax Research Foundation.

[36] Clements, K.W., Selvanathan, A. and Selvanathan, S. (1996) Applied demand analysis: a survey. *Economic Record*, 72, pp. 63-81.

[37] Conway, K.S. (1997) Labor supply, taxes, and government spending: a microeconometric analysis. *Review of Economic Studies*, LXXIX, pp. 50-67.

[38] Cornes, R. (1992) *Duality and Modern Economics*. Cambridge: Cambridge University Press.

[39] Cornwell, A. and Creedy, J. (1996) Carbon taxes, prices and inequality in Australia. *Fiscal Studies,* 17, pp. 21-38.

[40] Cornwell, A. and Creedy, J. (1997) *Environmental Taxes and Economic Welfare: Reducing Carbon Dioxide Emissions*. Aldershot: Edward Elgar.

[41] Cowling, K. and Mueller, D. (1978). The social costs of monopoly power. *Economic Journal*, 88, 727-748.

[42] Cornes, R. (1992) *Duality and Modern Economics.* Cambridge: Cambridge University Press.

[43] Creedy, J. (1992) *Income, Inequality and the Life Cycle.* Aldershot: Edward Elgar.

[44] Creedy, J. (1994) Taxes and transfers with endogenous earnings: some basic analytics. *Bulletin of Economic Research,* 46, pp. 97-130.

[45] Creedy, J. (1996) *Fiscal Policy and Social Welfare: An Analysis of Alternative Tax and Transfer Systems.* Aldershot: Edward Elgar.

[46] Creedy, J. (1997a) The distribution effects of indirect tax reform and inflation in New Zealand. *University of Melbourne Department of Economics Research Paper.*

[47] Creedy, J. (1997b) Taxation in general equilibrium: an introduction. *Bulletin of Economic Research* ,49, pp. 177-203.

[48] Creedy, J. (1998a) The optimal linear income tax: utility or equivalent income? *Scottish Journal of Political Economy,* 45, pp. 99-110.

[49] Creedy, J. (1998b) Measuring the welfare effects of price changes: a convenient parametric approach. *Australian Economic Papers* 37, pp. 136-150.

[50] Creedy, J. and Dixon, R. (1997) The distributional effects of monopoly. *University of Melbourne Department of Economics Research Paper,* no. 576.

[51] Creedy, J. and Dixon, R. (1998). The relative burden of monopoly on households with different incomes. *Economica,* (forthcoming).

[52] Creedy, J. and Martin, C. (1997) Estimates of the linear expenditure system using the 1993 Household Expenditure Survey. *University of Melbourne Institute of Applied Economic and Social Research Working Paper,* no. 12/97.

[53] Creedy, J. and van de Ven, J. (1997c) The distributional effects of inflation in Australia 1980-1995. *Australian Economic Review*, 30, pp. 125-143.

[54] Creel, M.D. (1997) Welfare estimation using the Fourier form: simulation evidence for the recreational demand case. *Review of Economics and Statistics*, LXXIX, pp. 88-94.

[55] Dahlby, B.G. (1977) The measurement of consumer surplus and the path dependence problem. *Public Finance*, 32, pp.293-311.

[56] Deaton, A.S. (1974) A reconsideration of the empirical implications of additive preferences. *Economic Journal*, 84, pp. 338-348.

[57] Deaton, A.S. (1975) *Models and Projections of Demand in Post-war Britain*. London: Chapman and Hall.

[58] Deaton, A.S. (1979) The distance function in consumer behaviour with applications to index numbers and optimal taxation. *Review of Economic Studies*, 46, pp. 391-405.

[59] Deaton, A. S. (1986) Demand analysis. In *Handbook of Econometrics*, Vol. III. (ed. by Z. Griliches and M. D. Intriligator), pp. 1768-1839. New York: North-Holland.

[60] Deaton, A.S. and Muellbauer, J. (1980) *Economics and Consumer Behaviour*. Cambridge: Cambridge University Press.

[61] Deaton, A.S. and Ng, S. (1996) Parametric and non-parametric approaches to price and tax reform. *National Bureau of Economic Research Working Paper*, no. 5564.

[62] Diamond, P.A. and McFadden, D.L. (1974) Some uses of the expenditure function in public finance. *Journal of Public Economics*, 3, pp. 3-21.

[63] Diewert, W.E. and Lawrence, D.A. (1994) *The Marginal Costs of Taxation in New Zealand*. Canberra: Swan Consultation.

[64] Dixon, P., Parmenter, B.R., Sutton, J. and Vincent, D. P. (1982) *ORANI: A Multisectoral Model of the Australian Economy.* Amsterdam: North-Holland.

[65] Dodgson, J. (1983) On the accuracy and appropriateness of alternative measures of excess burden. *Economic Journal,* 93 (Supp), pp. 105-113.

[66] Dower, R. and Zimmerman, M.B. (1992) *The Climate for Carbon Taxes: Creating Economic Incentives to Protect the Environment.* Washington DC: World Resources Institute.

[67] Due, J. (1988) The New Zealand goods and services (value added) tax – a model for other countries. *Canadian Tax Journal,* pp. 125-144.

[68] Dupuit, J. (1844) De la mésure de l'utilité des travaux publics. *Annales des ponts et chaussees, 8.* Translated and reprinted in *Readings in Welfare Economics* (ed. by K. Arrow and T. Scitovsky), 1969, pp. 255-283. New York: Allen and Unwin.

[69] Ebert, U. (1995) Consumer's surplus: simple solutions to an old problem. *Bulletin of Economic Research,* 47, pp. 285-294.

[70] Feldstein, M.S. (1972) Distributional equity and the optimal structure of public prices. *American Economic Review,* 62, pp. 32-36.

[71] Findlay, C.C. and Jones, R.L. (1982) The marginal cost of Australian income taxation. *The Economic Record,* 58, pp. 253-262.

[72] Fortin, B. and Lacroix, G. (1994) Labour supply, tax evasion and the marginal cost of public funds: an empirical investigation. *Journal of Public Economics,* 55, pp. 407-431.

[73] Fortin, B., Truchon, M. and Beauséjour, L. (1993) On reforming the welfare system: workfare meets the negative income tax. *Journal of Public Economics,* 51, pp. 119-151.

[74] Foster, C.D. and Neuburger, H.L.I. (1974) The ambiguity of the consumer's surplus measure of welfare change. *Oxford Economic Papers*, 26, pp. 66-77.

[75] Frantz, R. (1988) *X-efficiency: Theory, Evidence, and Applications*. Boston: Kluwer Academic Publishers.

[76] Freebairn, J. (1995) Reconsidering the marginal welfare cost of taxation. *Economic Record*, 71, pp. 121-131.

[77] Frisch, R. (1959) A complete system for computing all direct and cross demand elasticities in a model with many sectors. *Econometrica*, 27, pp. 177-196.

[78] Fullerton, D. (1991) Reconciling recent estimates of the marginal welfare cost of taxation. *American Economic Review*, 81, pp. 302-308.

[79] Goldberger, A.S. (1964) *Econometric theory*. Chichester: JohnWiley.

[80] Gravelle, H. and Rees, R. (1992) *Microeconomics*. London: Longman.

[81] Hammond, P.J. (1990) Theoretical progress in public economics: a provocative assessment. *Oxford Economic Papers*, 42, pp. 6-33.

[82] Harberger, A.C. (1964) Taxation, resource allocation and welfare. In *The Role of Direct and Indirect Taxes in the Federal Reserve System*. Princeton, NJ: Princeton University Press.

[83] Hause, J.C. (1975) The theory of welfare cost measurement. *Journal of Political Economy*, 83, pp. 1145-1182.

[84] Hausman, J.A. (1981) Exact consumer's surplus and deadweight loss. *American Economic Review*, 71, pp. 662-676.

[85] Hausman, J.A. (1985) The econometrics of nonlinear budget sets. *Econometrica*, 53, pp. 1255-1282.

[86] Hausman, J.A. and Newey, W.K. (1995) Nonparametric estimation of exact consumers surplus and deadweight loss. *Econometrica*, 63, pp. 1445-1476.

[87] Haveman, Robert H., Gabay, M. and Andreoni, J. (1987) Exact consumer's surplus and deadweight loss: a correction. *American Economic Review*, 77, pp. 494-495.

[88] Heady, C. (1993) Optimal taxation as a guide to tax policy: a survey. *Fiscal Studies*, 14, pp. 15-41.

[89] Industry Commission (1991) *Costs and Benefits of Reducing Greenhouse Gas Emissions*, Report no. 15. Canberra: Australian Government Publishing Service.

[90] Jenkin, F. (1871) On the principles which regulate the incidence of taxes. In *Readings in the Economics of Taxation* (ed. by R.A. Musgrave and C.S. Shoup), pp. 227-239. London: Allen and Unwin.

[91] Johansson, P-O. (1987) *The Economic Theory and Measurement of Environmental Benefits.* Cambridge: Cambridge University Press.

[92] Johnson, D., Freebairn, J., Creedy, J., Scutella, R. and Cowling, S. (1997) *A Stocktake of Taxation in Australia.* Melbourne: Melbourne Institute of Applied Economic and Social Research.

[93] Kay, J.A. (1980) The deadweight loss from a tax system. *Journal of Public Economics*, 13, pp. 111-119.

[94] Kay, J.A. (1983) A general equilibrium approach to the measurement of monopoloy welfare loss. *International Journal of Industrial Organisation*, 1, pp. 317-331.

[95] King, M.A. (1983) Welfare analysis of tax reforms using household data. *Journal of Public Economics*, 21, pp. 183-214.

[96] King, M.A. (1987) Empirical analysis of tax reforms. In *Advances in Econometrics,* Vol. II (ed. by T.F. Bewly). Cambridge: Cambridge University Press.

[97] Kolm, S.-Ch. (1976) Unequal inequalities: I and II. *Journal of Economic Theory,* 12, pp. 416-442 and 13, pp. 82-111.

[98] Lambert, P.J. (1985) Endogenizing the income distribution: the redistributive effect, and Laffer effects, of a progressive tax-benefit system. *European Journal of Political Economy,* 1, pp. 3-20.

[99] Lambert, P.J. (1993a) Evaluating impact effects of tax reforms. *Journal of Economic Surveys,* 7, pp. 205-242.

[100] Lambert, P.J. (1993b) *The Distribution and Redistribution of Income.* Manchester: Manchester University Press.

[101] Larson, D.M. (1988) Exact welfare measurement for producers under uncertainty. *American Journal of Agricultural Economics,* 70, pp. 597-603.

[102] Larson, D.M. (1992) Further results on willingness to pay for nonmarket goods. *Journal of Environmental Economics and Management,* 23, pp. 101-122.

[103] Lerner, A. (1934). The concept of monopoly and the measurement of monopoly power. *Review of Economic Studies,* 1, 157-175.

[104] Lluch, C., Powell, A. and Williams, R. (1977) *Patterns in Household Demand and Saving.* Oxford: Oxford University Press for the World Bank.

[105] Madden, D. (1995) An analysis of indirect tax reform in Ireland in the 1980s. *Fiscal Studies,* 16, pp. 18-37.

[106] Madden, D. (1996) Marginal tax reform and the specification of consumer demand systems. *Oxford Economic Papers.* 48, pp. 556-567.

[107] Madden, D. (1997) Conditional demand and marginal tax reform. *Oxford Bulletin of Economics and Statistics*, 59, pp. 237-255.

[108] Malmquist, S. (1993) Index numbers and demand functions. *Journal of Productivity Analysis*, 4, pp. 251-260.

[109] Marshall, A. (1961) *Principles Of Economics*. (9th edn ed. by C.W. Guillebaud). London: Macmillan.

[110] Mayshar, J. (1990) On measures of excess burden and their application. *Journal of Public Economics*, 43, pp. 263-290.

[111] Mayshar, J. and Yitzhaki, S. (1995) Dalton-improving indirect tax reform. *Americal Economic Review*, 85, pp. 793-807.

[112] McDougall, R.A. (1993) Short-run effects of a carbon tax. *Monash University Centre of Policy Studies and the IMPACT Project, General Paper, G-100*.

[113] McKenzie, G. (1983) *Measuring Economic Welfare: New Methods*. Cambridge: Cambridge University Press.

[114] McKeown, P.C. and Woodfield, A.E. (1995) The welfare cost of taxation in New Zealand following major tax reforms. *New Zealand Economic Papers*, 29, pp. 41-62.

[115] Mohring, H. (1971) Alternative welfare gain and loss measures. *Western Economic Journal*, 9, pp. 349-368.

[116] Muellbauer, J. (1974) Prices and inequality: the United Kingdom experience. *Economic Journal*, 84, pp. 32-55.

[117] Musgrave, R.A. (1959) *The Theory of Public Finance*. New York: McGraw-Hill.

[118] Newbery, D.M. (1995) The distributional impact of price changes in Hungary and the United Kingdom. *Economic Journal*, 105, pp. 847-863.

[119] Newbery, D.M. and Stern, N. (eds.) (1987) *The Theory of Taxation for Developing Countries*. Oxford University Press for the World Bank.

[120] Owen, A.D. (1992) *The Use of a Carbon Tax for Controlling Carbon Dioxide Emissions: Report prepared for the Department of the Arts, Sport, the Environment and Territories, Australia*. Canberra: Australian Government Publishing Services.

[121] Pauwels, W. (1986) Correct and incorrect measures of deadweight loss of taxation. *Public Finance*, 41, pp. 267-276.

[122] Pazner, E.A. and Sadka, E. (1980) Excess burden and economic surplus as consistent welfare indicators. *Public Finance*, 35, pp. 439-449.

[123] Pearce, D. (1991) The role of carbon taxes in adjusting to global warming. *Economic Journal*, 101, pp. 938-948.

[124] Pfingsten, A. (1987) Axiomatically-based local measures of tax progression. *Bulletin of Economic Research*, 39, pp. 211-223.

[125] Porter-Hudak, S. and Hayes, K. (1986) The statistical precision of a numerical methods estimator as applied to welfare loss. *Economics Letters*, 20, pp. 255-257.

[126] Porter-Hudak, S. and Hayes, K. (1987) Regional welfare loss measures of the 1973 oil embargo: a numerical methods approach. *Applied Economics*, 19, pp. 1317-1327.

[127] Powell, A.A. (1974) *Empirical Analytics of Demand Systems*. Lexington, Massachusetts: Lexington Books.

[128] Proops, J.L.R., Faber, M. and Wagenhals, G. (1993) *Reducing CO_2 Emissions: A Comparative Input-Output Study for Germany and the UK*. Heidelberg: Springer-Verlag.

[129] Rimmer, M.T. (1995) Development of a multi-household version of the Monash model. *Centre of Policy Studies, Monash University, Working Paper*, OP-81.

[130] Roberts, K. (1980) Price-independent welfare prescriptions. *Journal of Public Economics*, 18, pp. 277-297.

[131] Rosen, H.S. (1978) The measurement of excess burden with explicit utility functions. *Journal of Political Economy*, 86, pp. S121-S136

[132] Schob, R. (1994) On marginal cost and marginal benefit of public funds. *Public Finance*, 49, pp. 87-106.

[133] Scott, C., Goss, P. and Davis, H. (1985) *The Incidence of Indirect Taxes*, Vol. 1. Wellington: Victoria University Press.

[134] Scutella, R. (1997) The incidence of indirect taxes on final demand in Australia. *Melbourne Institute of Applied Economic and Social Research Working Paper*.

[135] Slesnick, D.T. (1990) Inflation, relative price variation, and inequality. *Journal of Econometrics*, 43, pp. 135-151.

[136] Slottje, D.J. (1987) Relative price changes and inequality in the size distribution of income. *Journal of Business and Economic Statistics*, 5, pp. 19-26

[137] Snow, A. and Warren, R.S. (1996) The marginal welfare cost of public funds: theory and estimates. *Journal of Public Economics*, 61, pp. 289-305.

[138] St John, S. (1993) Tax and welfare reforms in New Zealand. *Australian Economic Review*, 4'93, pp. 37-42.

[139] Stahl, D.O. (1985) A note on the consumer surplus path-of-integration problem. *Economica*, 50, pp. 95-98.

[140] Stephens, R.J. (1993) New Zealand's tax reform 1984-1992. In *Fightback! An Economic Assessment* (ed. by J.G. Head), pp. 193-242. Sydney: Australian Tax Foundation.

[141] Stern, N. (1976) On the specification of models of optimum income taxation. *Journal of Public Economics*, 6, pp. 123-162.

[142] Stigler, G. (1966) The statistics of monopoly and merger. *Journal of Political Economy*, 64, pp. 33-40.

[143] Stoker, T.M. (1986) The distributional welfare effects of rising prices in the United States: the 1970s experience. *American Economic Review*, 76, pp. 335-349.

[144] Stuart, C. (1984) Welfare cost per dollar of additional tax revenue in the United States. *American Economic Review*, 74, pp. 352-362.

[145] Symons, S., Proops, J. and Gay, P. (1994) Carbon taxes, consumer demand and carbon dioxide emissions: a simulation analysis for the UK. *Fiscal Studies*, 15(2), pp. 19-43.

[146] Triest, R.K. (1990) The relationship between the marginal cost of public funds and marginal excess burden. *American Economic Review*, 80, pp. 557-566.

[147] Tulpule, A. and Powell, A.A. (1978) Estimates of household demand elasticities for the Orani model. *Monash University IMPACT Project, Preliminary Working Paper, OP-22*.

[148] Usher, D. (1986) Tax evasion and the marginal cost of public funds. *Economic Inquiry*, 24, pp. 563-586.

[149] Varian, H. (1982) The nonparametric approach to demand analysis. *Econometrica*, 50, pp. 945-973.

[150] Varian, H. (1992) *Microeconomic Analysis*. New York: Norton.

[151] Vartia, Y.O. (1983) Efficient methods of measuring welfare change and compensated income in terms of demand functions. *Econometrica*, 51, pp. 79-98.

[152] Walker, I. (1993) Income taxation, income support policies and work incentives in the UK. In *Current Issues in Public Sector Economics* (ed. by P.M. Jackson), pp. 31-57. London: Macmillan.

[153] Wallace, S. and Wasylenko, M. (1992) Tax reform 1986 and marginal welfare changes for labor. *Southern Economic Journal*, 59, pp. 39-48.

[154] Waterson, M. (1984) *Economic Theory of the Industry.* Cambridge: Cambridge University Press.

[155] Weymark, J.A. (1980) Duality results in demand analysis. *European Economic Review,* 14, pp. 377-395.

[156] Wildasin, D.E. (1979) Public good provision with optimal and non-optimal commodity taxation. *Economic Letters*, 4, pp. 59-64.

[157] Williams, R. (1978). The use of disaggregated cross-section data in explaining shifts in Australian consumer demand patterns over time. *Monash University IMPACT Project, Preliminary Working Paper*, no. SP-13.

[158] Willig, R.D. (1976) Consumer's surplus without apology. *American Economic Review*, 66, pp. 589-597.

[159] Wright, B.D. and Williams J.C. (1988) Measurement of consumer gains from market stabilization. *American Journal of Agricultural Economics*, 70, pp. 616-627.

[160] Yitzhaki, S. (1983) On an extension of the Gini index. *International Economic Review*, 24, pp. 617-628.

[161] Youn Kim, H. (1997) Inverse demand systems and welfare measurement in quantity space. *Southern Economic Journal*, 63, pp. 663-679.

Index

219